ENGLISH FOR INTERNATIONAL
TOURISM

IWONNA DUBICKA · MARGARET O'KEEFFE

Pearson Education Limited
Edinburgh Gate
Harlow
Essex CM20 2JE
England
and Associated Companies throughout the world.

www.pearsonelt.com

First published 2013

ISBN: 978-1-4479-2387-9

Set in: Avenir Light 9.5/12.5pt
Printed by: Neografia, Slovakia

Acknowledgements

The publishers and authors would like to thank Dorling Kindersley for permission to use authentic material taken from the Eyewitness Travel Guides.

The publishers and authors would like to thank the following people and institutions for their feedback and comments during the development of the material:

Argentina: Lic. María Eugenia Pérez de Castro; **Austria:** Dr. Helga Vereno (TSS Klessheim, Salzburg), Mag. Ingrid Allesch (TSS Klessheim, Salzburg); **France:** Morene Schwartz Ach, Tonia Steciuk (Vatel International Business School Hotel & Tourism Management); **Italy:** Lesley Jane Ray; **Poland:** Jolanta Regucka-Pawlina (Cracow University of Economics); **Serbia:** Zorica Kovačević (IH Belgrade Syllabus); **Spain:** María Amparo González Rúa (Escuela Universitaria de Turismo de Asturias), María del Mar González Chacón (Escuela Universitaria de Turismo de Asturias); **Russia:** Tatyana Yefremtseva (Russian International Academy for Tourism)

'DK' and the DK 'open book' logo are trade marks of Dorling Kindersley Limited and are used in this publication under licence.

Author Acknowledgements

The authors would like to thank the following for their invaluable help during the project: Saverio Pergo, the air traffic control team in Barcelona, William Bain, Dave Hall, Susan Grove, María Alventosa García, Hotel Alga in Calella de Palafrugell, and Rafael Rocamora Abellan at the Escuela de Turismo, Universidad de Murcia.

We are grateful to the following for permission to reproduce copyright material:

Text

Extract on page 28 from Edinburgh Bus Tours, 2011, www.edinburghtour.com, Reproduced by permission of Lothian Buses plc, and 3x1 Public Relations; Extract on page 45 adapted from "Train Your Hospitality Team To Say "YES!" To Guest Complaints", http://www.hospitalitynet.org, 02/06/2010, p.3 (Doug Kennedy), copyright © Doug Kennedy. Reproduced with permission; Extract on page 78 adapted from 'Cost model: Hotel refurbishment', *Building Magazine*, Issue 23, 2002 (Davis Langdon & Everest), www.building.co.uk. Reproduced with permission of Building Magazine; Extract on page 79 adapted from "The Savoy reopens and a new era of luxury begins", *Fairmont Hotel Press Release*, October 2010, Reproduced by permission of Fairmont Hotels & Resorts, www.fairmont.com; Extract on page 80 adapted from 'GSA Handling Express Check-out Procedure' by Maximus, posted 8-26-2010 www.hotelmule.com. Reproduced with permission from HotelMule; Extract on page 103 about Our Dynamic Earth, www.dynamicearth.co.uk, copyright © Dynamic Earth Enterprises Ltd; Slogan on page 127: "Korea - be inspired", www.visitkorea.or.kr/, copyright © Korea Tourism Organization.

In some instances we have been unable to trace the owners of copyright material, and we would appreciate any information that would enable us to do so.

Illustration Acknowledgements

(Key: b-bottom; c-centre; l-left; r-right; t-top)

Kathy Baxendale 25, 43; 283 Tony (KJA Artists) 30–31

Picture Credits

The publisher would like to thank the following for their kind permission to reproduce their photographs:

(Key: b-bottom; c-centre; l-left; r-right; t-top)

Alamy Images: 23cr, AF archive 39cr, Blend Images 17tc, Chris Fredriksson 24t, Consignum 25cr, David Lyons 79bc, David R. Frazier Photolibrary, Inc. 72t, Don Campbell 17tr, Greg Balfour Evans 12t, Ilene MacDonald 22bl, Image Source 80t, Jan Wlodarczyk 65br, Juergen Henkelmann Photography 46cr, Li Ding 8t, Mark Karrass 82cr, Martin Beddall 20l, PhotoSpin 73br, Steve Vidler 17tl, Tommy Trenchard 50b; **Brand X Pictures:** 14bc; **Corbis:** Danny Lehman 34br, De Leo, Joseph 56b, Franz Neumayr / epa 38tr, Gavin Hellier / JAI 89b, Gianni Dagli Orti 33cr, Gunter Marx 30cl, Hall / photocuisine 54c, Helen King 43bc, Hussenot / photocuisine 52t, John E Marriott / All Canada Photos 4tl, 30cr, K.J. Historical 86tl, Ken Welsh / Design Pics 81br, Martin Ruetschi / Keystone 5tc, 26cr, Mascarucci 56cl, Ocean 53cr, 62cl, Ocean 53cr, 62cl, Paul A. Souders 93b, Paul Panayiotou 92t, Philippe Roy / Hemis 38br, Radius Images 20cl, Rob Howard 5bc, 63b, Stephan Zirwes / fstop 68t, Swim Ink 2, LLC 87br, Tomas Rodriguez 35cr, Topic Photo Agency 85cr; **Digital Vision:** 14cl; **DK Images:** 10t, 14c, 26c, 34bc, 38cr, 58cr, 58-59c, 62-63c, 66r, 82c, 90c, 90cr; **Fotolia.com:** 4cl, 4bl, 9br, 10tl, 10tr, 14tl, 14tr, 14b, 22br, 23t, 23tr, 32l, 32cr, 46cl, 58br, 61br, 64t, 66tc, 75b, 16, 18, 22tl, 17, 19, 21, 23tr, 24, 24, 30tl, 25, 27, 29, 31tr, 32, 34, 38tl, 33, 35, 37, 39tr, 41, 43, 45, 47tr, 52, 54, 58tl, 53, 55, 57, 59tr, 60, 62, 66tl, 61, 63, 65, 67tr, 68, 70, 74tl, 8,10,14tl, 84, 86, 90tl, 85, 87, 89, 91tr, 9,11,13,15tr; **Getty Images:** A & L Sinibaldi 48t, AFP 79bl, Allan Baxter 36t, Antenna Audio, Inc. 26tl, Bilderlounge 20t, ColorBlind Images 19br, Dex 32t, Digital Vision 18cl, 66c, Erik Simonsen 74-75c, Glowimages 34bl, John Warburton-Lee 63tc, Kevin Schafer 60t, Mitchell Funk 11b, Monty Rakusen 70t, Nick White 54cl, Pawel Libera 32cl, Reza Estakhrian 40t, Robert Daly 35br, UpperCut Images 13b; **Lonely Planet Images:** 61cr, Andrew Watson 90br, Karl Blackwell 37b, Peter Ptschelinzew 82cl; **Pearson Education Ltd:** 16t; **PhotoDisc:** 56l; **Rex Features:** James Fraser 28t; **Robert Harding World Imagery:** 34b, Arcaid 78t, Mike Watson / moodboard 101b, Nick Gibson / age fotostock 4-5c, Pete Ryan / National Geographic 26tr, Sergio Pitamitz 84t; **Shutterstock.com:** 32c, 40, 42, 46tl, 69, 71, 73, 75tr, 76, 78, 80, 82tl, 77, 79, 81, 83tr; **SNUBA® is a registered trademark of SNUBA International, Inc. Photo courtesy of SNUBA International, Inc. :** 66br; **StockFood UK:** Heath Robbins 56bl; **SuperStock:** 43bl, 88t, age fotostock 10tc, 63cl, age fotostock 10tc, 63cl, Axiom Photographic Limited 5cr, 26cl, 90tr, Axiom Photographic Limited 5cr, 26cl, 90tr, Belinda Images 4br, 38c, Glow Images 51br, Hemis.fr 76t, InsideOut Pix 52b, Kaehler, Wolfgang 62tc, Stock Connection 94bl, The Francis Frith Collection 44t, Travelshots 95b

Cover images: *Front:* **4Corners Images:** Benedetta Rusconi / SIME t; **Corbis:** F.Stuart Westmorland b, Jon Hicks bc; **SuperStock:** Fancy Collection tc; *Back:* **DK Images:** cl; **Fotolia.com:** tl; **Lonely Planet Images:** Peter Ptschelinzew bl

All other images © Pearson Education

Every effort has been made to trace the copyright holders and we apologise in advance for any unintentional omissions. We would be pleased to insert the appropriate acknowledgement in any subsequent edition of this publication.

INTRODUCTION

English for International Tourism is a three-level series designed to meet the English language needs of professionals working in the tourism industry and students of tourism in further education. The course includes authentic material taken from Dorling Kindersley's acclaimed *Eyewitness Travel Guides* which explore some of the world's top tourist destinations. The course helps you to:

- build confidence in professional skills such as dealing with enquiries, marketing destinations, offering advice, negotiating, writing emails and speaking to groups
- develop language awareness through an integrated grammar and skills syllabus
- acquire the specialized vocabulary needed by tourism professionals
- practise language skills in realistic Case studies that reflect issues in the tourist industry today.

Structure of the Coursebook

The Coursebook contains ten units and two Review and consolidation sections. Each unit is divided into four lessons. The Unit Menu shows you the key learning objective of the lesson. Each unit has the same structure:

- a vocabulary lesson
- a grammar lesson
- a Professional skills lesson
- a Case study or tourism-related game.

KEY VOCABULARY

The vocabulary lessons introduce and practise many words and expressions required in the tourism industry introduced either through a reading text or a listening. By the end of the lesson you will be better able to use the specialist vocabulary in appropriate tourism contexts. At the end of each unit there is a Key Word box that provides a selection of words and phrases from the unit and a reference to the Mini-dictionary on the DVD-ROM.

KEY GRAMMAR

In the grammar lessons key aspects of grammar that are essential for progress at this level are presented within an authentic tourism context. These lessons include clear explanations and activities designed to help you understand and use the language effectively. By the end of the lesson you will be able to use the grammar more confidently. For additional support there is a comprehensive Grammar reference at the back of the Coursebook.

PROFESSIONAL SKILLS

The Professional skills lessons provide you with the opportunity to learn and practise effective interpersonal and business skills which are an essential job requirement in the travel and tourism industries. You will learn professional skills ranging from dealing with customer enquiries and meeting clients' needs to preparing a guided tour or a presentation.

CASE STUDIES

Each unit ends with a Case study linked to the unit's tourism theme. The Case studies are based on realistic tourism issues or situations and are designed to motivate and actively engage you in seeking solutions. They use the language and professional skills which you have acquired while working through the unit and involve you in discussing the issues and recommending solutions through active group work.

Language skills

Speaking skills: Each unit provides you with a range of speaking activities. The pairwork tasks are designed to provide you with further opportunities to communicate in realistic and motivating tourism-related contexts. The Case studies require you to engage in extended communication about topical issues in the tourism industry. At each level further speaking practice is available in a tourism-related board game.

Listening skills: Each unit contains several listening tasks developed around topics related to the travel industry. A range of British, American and other international native and non-native speakers are featured helping you understand how people speak English in different parts of the world. Audio scripts of the recordings are available at the back of the Coursebook.

Reading practice: Reading texts feature regularly in the units providing you with a variety of texts and topics that you are likely to encounter in a tourism context.

Writing practice: In the writing sections you will write real texts related to the tourism workplace such as emails, tour itineraries. At each level there are also writing tasks to help you get a job in tourism. Models of text types are available in the Writing Bank at the back of the Coursebook.

Workplace skills

Working with numbers: Throughout the course there are sections that help you to manipulate numbers in English, which is a vital skill in the travel and tourism workplace.

Research tasks: Each unit contains one or more research tasks that encourage you to explore tourism-related issues on the internet or in your local environment.

Private study

Workbook: A separate Workbook with a CD provides you with extra tasks for study at home or in class. There are two versions of the Workbook – one with the answer key for private study and one without a key which can be used by the teacher for extra practice in class.

DVD-ROM: The course has a DVD-ROM designed to be used alongside the Coursebook or as a free-standing video for private study. The DVD-ROM is attached to the back of the Coursebook and provides you with five authentic films featuring different aspects of tourism. Each film has a printable worksheet, a transcript and a key to the exercises. These films give you the opportunity to listen to a variety of native and non-native speakers using English as an international language in five authentic documentary videos. Additionally, the DVD-ROM has a comprehensive Mini-dictionary featuring over 300 tourism-related terms along with their definitions, pronunciation and example sentences. The DVD-ROM also contains the MP3 files of the Coursebook audio material.

Professional exams

English for International Tourism is recommended preparation for the LCCI English for tourism exams www.lcci.org.uk

WORLD MAP

Canada p. 30–31

FILM C

USA p. 10–11

New England, USA p. 82–83

London, England p. 32–33

FILM B

Cancún, Mexico p. 34–35

Costa Rica p. 60–61

Barcelona, Spain p. 36–37

Peru p. 14–15

Austria p. 38–39

DVD-ROM FILMS

- **A** Dream Holidays
- **B** Cycling in Paris
- **C** Kilworth House
- **D** Sea Kayaking in the Hebrides
- **E** Movie Tourism in New Zealand

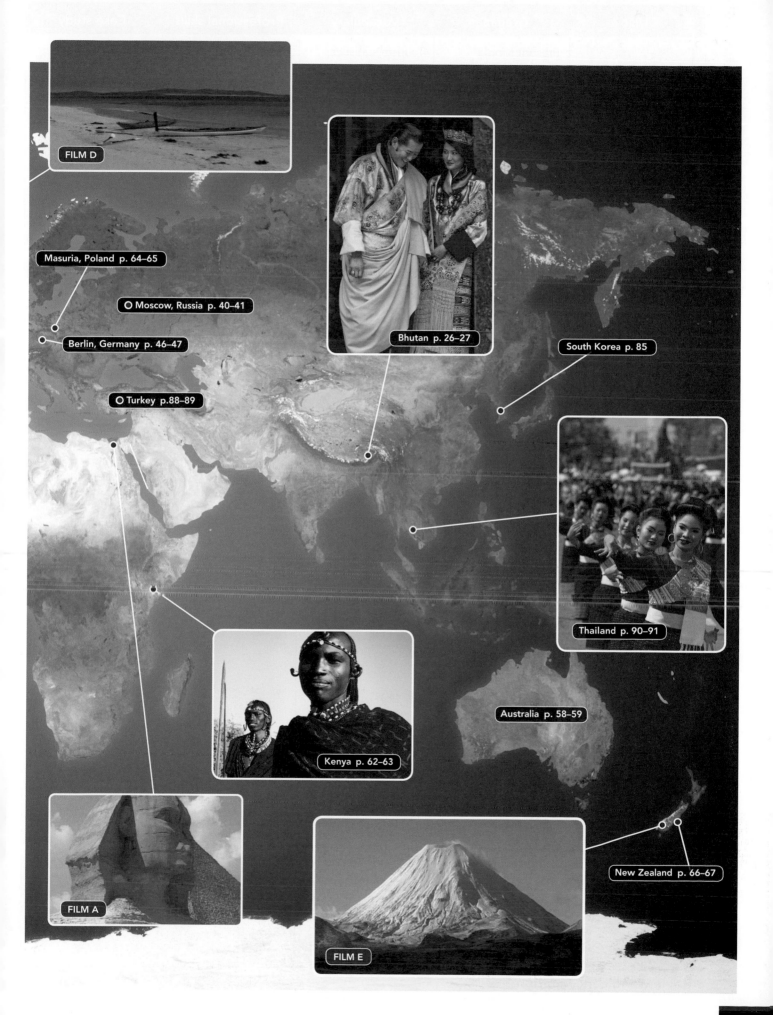

FILM D

Masuria, Poland p. 64–65

○ Moscow, Russia p. 40–41

Berlin, Germany p. 46–47

○ Turkey p.88–89

Bhutan p. 26–27

South Korea p. 85

Thailand p. 90–91

Kenya p. 62–63

Australia p. 58–59

FILM A

FILM E

New Zealand p. 66–67

CONTENTS

1

WORLD TOURISM

UNIT MENU

Grammar: present simple question forms
Vocabulary: tourism statistics
Professional skills: checking and confirming details
Case study: make the right booking

Speaking

TOURIST DESTINATIONS

1 **What are the world's top tourist destinations? Put the countries in order from 1 to 6. Compare your ideas with a partner. Then check your answers in File 1 on page 102.**

> China   France   Italy   Spain
> United Kingdom (the UK)   United States of America (the USA)

Reading

THE TOURISM INDUSTRY

2 **Read the tourism industry facts. Match the key words and phrases 1–8 with the definitions a–h.**

> Tourism is one of the world's biggest industries, and the World Tourism Organization (WTO) expects it to continue growing by four percent a year.

> Germany, the USA and China are the countries that spend the most on outbound tourism all over the world. Other top spenders are the UK, France and Canada.

> Most tourism in the world is domestic tourism – people travelling in their own country. It represents about 80 percent of all tourist trips today.

> People travel for many reasons. Some inbound tourists travel for leisure, recreation and holidays. Other people are visiting friends and relatives (VFR) or travelling for health and religious reasons. Others travel for business and professional purposes.

1 inbound tourism	**a** a member of your family
2 outbound tourism	**b** people travelling in their own country
3 domestic tourism	**c** travel for a short time or for a specific reason
4 VFR stands for	**d** tourists arriving in different countries from their own
5 trip	**e** time devoted to rest, relaxation and pleasure
6 relative	**f** visiting friends and relatives
7 leisure	**g** to give money as a payment for something
8 spend	**h** tourists visiting places outside their own country

Vocabulary

NUMBERS

3 **))) 1.1** **Listen and practise saying the numbers.**

1 1 to 20

2 21, 32, 43, 54, 65, 76, 87, 98

3 109, 210, 311, 412, 513, 620, 730, 840, 950

4 1,000, 1,500, 10,000, 10,750, 100,000, 1,000,000, 1,000,000,000

4 **))) 1.2** **Listen and circle the number you hear. Then practise saying the numbers.**

1 13, 30   **2** 14, 40   **3** 15, 50   **4** 16, 60   **5** 17, 70   **6** 18, 80   **7** 19, 90

5 **))) 1.3** **Complete the table. Then listen and check your answers.**

Percentages	Fractions	Decimals
1 150%	1 _____	1.5
2 75%	¾	2 _____
3 3 _____	½	0.5
4 33.3%	4 _____	0.33
5 25%	¼	5 _____
6 6 _____	⅕	0.2
7 12½%	⅛	7 _____
8 10%	8 _____	0.1

Listening

TOURISM STATISTICS

6 **))) 1.4** **Work in pairs. What do you know about international tourism? Discuss these questions. Then listen and check your answers.**

1 Which continent receives the most visitors?

2 Which country receives the most money (receipts) from international tourism?

3 Which nation spends the most on travel and tourism?

4 Which country does the WTO expect to be the world's top destination within the next five years?

Vocabulary

TOURISM SECTORS

7 **Match the tourism sectors 1–7 with the words and phrases a–g. Use a dictionary if necessary. Add at least TWO more words/phrases to each sector.**

1 Accommodation   **a** Olympic Games, business convention

2 Recreation and entertainment   **b** travel agent, tour operator

3 Attractions   **c** restaurant, café

4 Events and conferences   **d** zoo, museum

5 Food and beverage   **e** airline, railway

6 Transportation   **f** campsite, bed and breakfast

7 Travel trades   **g** golf, skiing

8 **Which sector do you work in, or would you like to work in? Which sectors generate the most jobs and money in your country?**

> **RESEARCH**
>
> TOURISM IN YOUR COUNTRY
> Find out five key facts and figures about the tourism industry in your country and present them to the class. Think about domestic, inbound and outbound tourism.

THE UNITED STATES

Speaking

THE GREAT USA QUIZ

1 Match the photos of places in the USA with the names in the box. What do you know about these places? Compare your ideas with a partner.

> Las Vegas   San Francisco   The Grand Canyon   Times Square

2 Study the Grammar box below and complete the questions in the quiz. Use the question words and phrases in the box. Not all the words and phrases are needed.

> how   how long   how many   how much   how often   how old
> what   when   where   which   who   why

The Great USA Quiz

1 ¹_____ are most international visitors to the USA from?
  a Canada   **b** the UK   **c** Mexico

2 ²_____ does the typical visitor spend during their visit to the USA?
  a $2,000   **b** $3,000   **c** $3,500

3 ³_____ does the average international tourist stay in the USA?
  a 12 nights   **b** 16 nights   **c** 21 nights

4 ⁴_____ is the top tourist attraction in the USA?
  a Disney World, Florida   **b** Las Vegas, Nevada   **c** Times Square, New York

5 ⁵_____ international tourists does the top attraction receive every year?
  a 3 million   **b** 7 million   **c** 37 million

6 There are seven natural wonders of the world. ⁶_____ one is in the USA?

7 ⁷_____ do you say the American English words *vacation*, *cab*, *elevator*, *restroom* in British English?

8 ⁸_____ do people celebrate Thanksgiving Day in the USA?
  a the fourth Thursday in November   **b** 4 July   **c** 31 December

3 Work in pairs. Complete the quiz. Then check your answers in File 2 on page 102.

GRAMMAR: PRESENT SIMPLE QUESTION FORMS

To form questions with **be**, change the order of the verb and the subject.
Is he American? ***Are you*** ready?
What is/What's the capital of the USA?

To form questions with other verbs, use the auxiliary verb **do/does**. The main verb stays in the infinitive form.
Form: question word + *do/does* + subject + infinitive
Do you ***like*** New York? ***Does*** he ***speak*** English?
When does the flight ***leave***?

See Grammar reference, page 112.

Reading

INTERNATIONAL TOURISTS IN THE USA

4 **What do you think are the top three activities of visitors to the USA? Compare your ideas with a partner.**

5 **Read the report on tourism in the USA and check your answers.**

International tourists in the USA

What does the typical international visitor do when he or she arrives in the USA? In a new survey, more than 50% of foreign visitors say that shopping is their number one activity while visiting the USA. According to the survey of 2,500 foreign tourists, most visitors spend about $3,500 per person during their trip. They spend about a third of the money in retail stores – mostly on clothes. A typical shopping trip includes going to Macy's or JC Penney to look at the Levi's, Ralph Lauren and Diesel **merchandise**, and then eating at McDonald's. These **retailers** and **brands** are the most popular with tourists and the most widely recognized. New York was the number one shopping **destination** followed by Los Angeles, Las Vegas and Atlanta.

The survey focused on visitors from five countries: Australia and South Korea – which are **growth markets** for inbound tourism in the USA – and Brazil, China and India, which are **emerging markets**. There was also a second survey of visitors from Canada, Mexico, the UK, Japan and Germany, which are the current top five markets for inbound tourism. Both surveys gave surprisingly similar results.

After shops, the second most popular destination was parks – both natural parks and theme parks. Visiting museums, zoos and aquariums came next, and then eating out and going to concerts and theaters.

6 **Complete the sentences with the correct form of a word or phrase in bold in the report in Exercise 5.**

1 The _____ in the shop was very high quality.

2 Häagen-Dazs and Ben & Jerry's are _____ of ice cream.

3 The Caribbean is a popular _____ with tourists from both the USA and the UK.

4 Tiffany's is a luxury _____ in New York.

5 As more people travel there is a(n) _____ for low-cost airlines.

6 China is one of the biggest _____ for inbound tourism in the USA.

7 **Prepare a survey to find out more about tourism in your country. Put the questions 1–8 in the correct order.**

1 on / how / you / holiday / do / go / often

2 travel / do / how / usually / you

3 go / usually / you / do / where

4 usually / do / stay / you / where

5 you / long / do / go / for / how

6 do / with / who / go / you

7 do / do / what / on / you / holiday

8 spend / what / do / on / most / money / you

8 **Interview at least five other students in the class. Ask the survey questions you prepared in Exercise 7. Then prepare a summary of the results.**

PROFESSIONAL SKILLS
CHECKING AND CONFIRMING DETAILS

Listening

TELEPHONE MESSAGES

1))) **1.5** **Listen to three telephone calls and complete the messages with dates and times.**

1

> Table for six on ¹_____ at ²_____.

2

> Coach leaves Gdańsk on ³_____ at ⁴_____ in the morning.

3

> Two twin rooms with bath at the Palma Marina from the ⁵_____ to ⁶_____ July.

2 **What different ways are there for saying the dates and times in Exercise 1? Look at File 3 on page 102.**

3 **Work in pairs. Answer the questions.**

  1 Can you say today's date in two ways?

  2 What's the time now? Can you say it in two ways?

  3 Which months have 30 days and which have 31 days?

  4 Can you say the days of the week backwards?

  5 What is your favourite day of the week and your favourite month of the year? Why?

Speaking

EXPRESSIONS AND SPELLING

4))) **1.6** **Listen to two conversations and tick (✓) the expressions when you hear them. Listen again and write the email addresses.**

  1 _____ Can you repeat that, please?   **4** _____ That's all one word.

  2 _____ Double 'S'.   **5** _____ So, that's ...?

  3 _____ That's right.   **6** _____ That's 'S' for sugar.

5 **Work in pairs. Take turns to spell the following using the expressions in Exercise 4.**

  1 the address and email address of your organization

  2 the name and email address of a friend

  3 the address of your bank

Listening

A TELEPHONE BOOKING

6))) 1.7 Listen to Part One of a telephone booking and circle the correct option in italics.

1 The booking is for more than *20 / 30 / 40* people.

2 It is a *musical / sports event.*

3 The event is in *October / November / December.*

7))) 1.8 Listen to Part Two and complete the booking information.

London theatre reservations

Show: ¹_____
Date: ²_____ October
Time of performance: ³_____
Name of theatre: Lyceum Theatre, London
No. of tickets: ⁴_____

Ticket price: ⁵£_____
Name for booking: Vic ⁶_____
Payment method: ⁷_____
Credit card number: 4593 7688 ⁸_____ ⁹_____
Email address: ¹⁰_____

8 Complete the expressions in the Professional skills box. Look at audio scripts 1.7 and 1.8 on page 118 and check your answers.

PROFESSIONAL SKILLS: CHECKING AND CONFIRMING DETAILS

Checking:
¹_____ that E for Echo?
²_____, did you say double nine-O-two?
Can I just ³_____ the booking before I put the payment through?

Confirming:
Yes, that's ⁴_____
⁵_____ 34 seats for 16th October.
We'll send you an email ⁶_____ your booking.

Correcting:
No, *thirty*-four. ⁷_____, four.
Actually, it's Victor, ⁸_____ Vic.

Speaking

TAKING DETAILS ON THE TELEPHONE

9 Work in pairs. Student A turn to File 4, page 102. Student B turn to File 38, page 111. Practise taking booking details over the telephone. Use the expressions in the Professional skills box to help you.

Writing

CONFIRMING A BOOKING

10 Write an email to confirm the booking you made in Exercise 9. Use the model in the Writing bank on page 99 to help you.

CASE STUDY
MAKE THE RIGHT BOOKING

CASE STUDY MENU

Aim: To design and confirm a vacation package for a customer.

1 Listen to a telephone call and complete the customer's profile.
2 Read about and discuss the best holiday package choices.
3 Read messages and listen to changes to the customer's needs.
4 Make changes to the booking and confirm with the customer.
5 Confirm the booking and cost in writing.

Population	nearly 28 million
Located	tropical Andes
Capital	Lima
Official language(s)	Spanish and Quechua
Places of interest	Lima, Machu Picchu, Cusco, trekking on the Inca trail, ancient lines at Nazca, Lake Titicaca and the Amazon jungle
Best time to go	in winter from June to August when it's dry and sunny in the mountains and jungle

PERU

1 **Look at the information and photos of Peru. What is unusual about the country?**

Customer profile

2))) 1.9 **Gabi Werner works for CSAM Travel in Mexico City. Listen to a telephone call and complete the customer profile.**

Customer profile

Name: Mark [1]_____
Destination: [2]_____
Interests: trekking and local culture
Places to visit: [3]_____, the Amazon and [4]_____ Titicaca

Travelling with: [5]_____
Travel dates: [6]_____
10-day package: US[7]$_____
Email: mark.bradford@leeds. [8]_____

Choosing a package

3 Work in pairs. Look at the holiday packages and choose the best package for Mark. Write down the important details of the booking: the package choice, travel dates and total cost.

A Incan Wonders

(15 days/14 nights)
Arrival to Lima & Lima Tour – Paracas & Nazca Lines Tour – Return to Lima – Flight to Cusco and tour of Cusco, the Incan capital – Sacred Valley Tour – Trekking on the Inca Trail (five days) – Tour of Machu Picchu, one of the seven wonders of the world – Arrival to Puerto Maldonado – Amazon Tour (five days) – Departure from Puerto Maldonado – US $1,700 pp.

B The Land of the Incas

(Seven days/six nights)
Go on the Inca Trail and see Machu Picchu, the most famous archaeological site in South America – Arrival to Cusco and Cusco Tour – Sacred Valley Tour – Begin the Inca Trail Trek (three days) – Machu Picchu Tour and return to Cusco – Departure from Cusco – US $1,050 pp.

C Andean Adventures

(Four days/three nights)
Can be combined with other tours (add one extra day for travel) – Arrival to Cusco – Home stay accommodation at Lake Titicaca, the highest lake in the world (three days) – Cusco and Tour of Cusco – Departure from Cusco – US $500 pp.

D Peru Special

(Ten days/nine nights)
From ancient Incan ruins to the Amazon jungle – Arrival in Lima and Lima Tour – Flight to Cusco – Sacred Valley Tour – Trekking on the Inca Trail (three days) – Machu Picchu, the lost city of the Incas – Puerto Maldonado – Amazon tour with guided walks (three days) – Departure from Puerto Maldonado – US $1,200 pp.

TASK

4))) 1.10 Listen to Gabi calling Mark and make a note of any changes to his booking.

5))) Look at these optional tours. Listen again and choose one for Mark's Peru package.

6 Work in pairs. Student A turn to File 5, page 102. Student B turn to File 14, page 105.

Optional tours

1 Mountain train journey from Huancayo to Lima – 12-hour ride – Weekends only, June to September – US $40 pp.
2 (One day) Sand-boarding on the sand dunes in Huacachina – Four hours from Lima – US $55 pp.
3 (One day) Ancient Nazca lines in the desert – Tour from Paracas – US $125 pp.

Confirming a booking

7 Write an email to Mark to confirm his booking (100–120 words). Use the expressions in the box and the model in the Writing bank on page 99 to help you.

> Here is/are …   I would also like to confirm …
> Thank you for booking with …   Please see the attached details.
> Your booking includes …

UNIT 1: KEY WORDS

accommodation   booking
domestic tourism
inbound/outbound tourism
include   leisure   lower case
package   recreation
shopping   spend   theme park
trekking   trip
See DVD-ROM Mini-dictionary

2

JOBS IN TOURISM

UNIT MENU

Grammar: present simple and continuous

Vocabulary: working conditions and salaries, qualities and skills, hotel jobs

Professional skills: covering letters

Case study: choose the right person for the job

Reading

WORKING CONDITIONS IN TOURISM

1 Read the article and write down the advantages and disadvantages of working in the tourism industry.

Advantages	Disadvantages
e.g. *interesting and varied work*	e.g. *seasonal work, short-term contracts*

The truth about working in tourism

The main problem with the travel and tourism sector is that there is a lot of **seasonal** work on short-term contracts. The hours are sometimes long and hard, and many people consider working in tourism as a **temporary** option before they find jobs in other industries.

The positive aspect is that the work is often interesting and varied. Tourism is a people-focused industry, which offers the opportunity to meet and help people from all over the world. Tourism professionals often say that every day is different and you never know what to expect.

Working **shifts** and weekends is common but there is also more flexibility with working hours than in other industries. You can work **part-time** or full-time, night or day to suit your needs and interests. Tourism jobs can also be **low-paid** at the start but many hotel and travel organizations offer on-the-job training. Employees can earn a salary while they are learning practical skills they need to advance in the industry.

Many companies like their employees to start at the bottom to gain experience. If you work hard and develop the right skills, there can be opportunities for fast promotion. It is possible to have an interesting **long-term** career in tourism, and with a university degree you move more quickly into a management position.

2 Match the expressions 1–6 with their opposites in **bold** in the text in Exercise 1. Use a dictionary to help you.

1 full-time _____   3 high-paid _____   5 all year round _____

2 permanent _____   4 short-term _____   6 regular daytime hours _____

3 Match the jobs in the box with the correct sector of the tourist industry 1–4. Add at least TWO more jobs to each sector.

> concierge   entertainer   flight attendant   hotel receptionist
> outdoor adventure guide   pilot   restaurant manager   waiter

1 Food and beverage   3 Transportation

2 Accommodation   4 Recreation and entertainment

Listening

PERSONAL QUALITIES AND SKILLS

4))) 2.1 **Listen to three tourism professionals talking about their jobs. Match the personal qualities and skills in the box with each person.**

> customer-focused and efficient   energetic, enthusiastic and entertaining
> organized and communicative

1 Sumalee, travel agent: _____

2 Sandra, flight attendant: _____

3 Dev, tour guide: _____

5 (((**Complete the job descriptions 1–3 with the words in the box. Listen again and check your answers.**

> customer service   IT   sales

1 A **travel agent** needs to have excellent ^{1}_____ skills. He or she also needs good ^{2}_____ skills to sell holiday and travel products to customers. And, of course, good ^{3}_____ skills are essential to find information and make bookings online.

> communicator   first aid   team

2 A **flight attendant** needs to be a good ^{4}_____ who can interact with people from other cultures and be a good ^{5}_____ worker. Basic ^{6}_____ and medical skills are important.

> fun   organizational   passion

3 A **tour guide** needs to have a(n) ^{7}_____ for people. You need to be energetic because your job is about helping people to have ^{8}_____. Good ^{9}_____ skills and languages are also important.

6))) 2.2 **Listen and make notes on the salaries and working conditions for each person. Who has the best job in your opinion?**

Speaking

THE SKILLS FOR THE JOB

7 **Answer the questions. Compare your ideas with a partner.**

1 Which qualities and skills are the most important for your career in tourism?

2 Which qualities and skills do you want to develop in the future?

RESEARCH

JOB ADVERTS
Visit an English website advertising jobs in tourism. Find three jobs that you would like to do. What are the salaries? What personal qualities and skills do the adverts say you need for each job?

A DAY IN THE LIFE

Reading

YOU NEVER STOP LEARNING

1 **Complete the descriptions about hotel jobs with the correct job title in the box. What other hotel jobs can you think of?**

> executive chef   executive housekeeper
> food and beverage manager   front office manager   hotel receptionist

1 _____: plans and organizes the operations of a restaurant

2 _____: responsible for the front desk operations, managing reception and dealing with guests' problems

3 _____: makes reservations and checks guests in/out

4 _____: writes menus, instructs cooks and employs kitchen staff

5 _____: inspects rooms and manages cleaning staff

2 **Nathan Wilson works in a busy hotel in Vancouver, Canada. Read the article and complete it with the correct job title from Exercise 1.**

A Day in the Life ... Nathan Wilson of the Bouvier Hotel

Nathan works for the Bouvier Hotel chain in Vancouver. As a ¹_____, he manages twelve front office staff and also deals with guests all day. 'If a guest has a problem or an unusual request, it's my job to help them,' says Nathan. 'I'm the official "face" of the hotel for guests and it's up to me to make sure that they walk out of the door feeling happy.' People management skills are important in his job. He is responsible for the reception, concierge and bell service staff and organizes their shifts and work schedules. He also recruits new employees and organizes staff training.

Nathan loves his job because 'You never stop learning.' As well as front desk work, he often works on pricing and promotions with the marketing department and negotiates with corporate clients for conferences and banquet services. This month, he is helping to develop a new online promotion. 'If you work in hotels, there's always something new to learn. I started out with a qualification in hospitality. After I finished my diploma, I started at the bottom as a prep cook. Later, I became a sous chef and after that, an executive chef. But then I realized I love dealing with guests and I got interested in front office work.'

Although he doesn't work in the kitchen these days, Nathan still has a passion for cooking and for travel. His dream is to become General Manager of one of Bouvier Hotels, and work abroad.

3 **Read the text in Exercise 2 again and complete Nathan's profile.**

Name: Nathan Wilson
Age: 34
Marital status: married, two children
Main responsibilities:
- managing ¹_____
- organizing ²_____
- dealing with ³_____
- negotiating with ⁴_____
- recruitment and training new employees

Qualifications: a diploma in ⁵_____
Previous jobs: ⁶_____, ⁷_____, ⁸_____
Hobbies and interests: ⁹_____
Future career plans: ¹⁰_____

GRAMMAR: PRESENT SIMPLE AND CONTINUOUS

Use the **present simple** to talk about facts and situations that are generally true.
Nathan **supervises** front office staff and **deals with** guests all day.
You never **stop** learning.

Use the **present continuous** to describe current projects and temporary events.
I**'m learning** new things today/this morning/week/month.
What **are** you **working on** at the moment/now?

See Grammar reference, pages 112 and 113.

4 Study the Grammar box and read the text in Exercise 2 again. What is Nathan Wilson working on at the moment?

5 Complete the sentences 1–8 with the verbs in brackets in the present simple or continuous.

1 At the moment, I [1]_____ (train) two new front desk clerks.

2 At present, I'm supervising them on the job. I [2]_____ (help) them to learn about accommodation services.

3 It [3]_____ (be) very important they know how to deal with customer complaints.

4 I [4]_____ (be) also [5]_____ (show) our new staff how our reservation system [6]_____ (work).

5 They [7]_____ (find) that difficult because it isn't one they normally [8]_____ (use).

6 Currently, I [9]_____ (plan) a trip to the lakes with my family.

7 I [10]_____ (not) usually [11]_____ (take) holidays during the busy season so I [12]_____ (be) a bit nervous.

8 I need to make sure my assistant [13]_____ (know) what she has to do before I go!

6 Use the prompts to make sentences about what other staff at the Bouvier Hotel do and what they are doing at the moment.

e.g. *The executive chef manages the kitchen staff. At the moment, she's planning the menu for a banquet.*

1 executive chef: manage kitchen staff/plan menu for a banquet

2 receptionist: work front desk/check in group of 25

3 executive housekeeper: supervise cleaning staff/inspect all bathrooms

4 building manager: look after building/supervise repair work

5 waiter: wait at tables/take lunch order

6 bell boy: help guests with luggage/carry heavy bag

Speaking

20 QUESTIONS GAME

7 Work in pairs to play the 20 questions game. Think of a job. Your partner can ask up to 20 *Yes/No* questions to guess what it is. Then swap roles and guess your partner's job.

A: Do you usually work in the kitchen?   *B:* Yes, I do.

A: Are you preparing food for the chef at the moment?   *B:* No, I'm not.

PROFESSIONAL SKILLS
COVERING LETTERS

Reading

JOB ADVERTISEMENTS

1 Complete the job adverts with the best word or expression in italics.

JOB OPPORTUNITIES AT FUN PARKS

Fun Parks are offering temporary and permanent ¹*positions/job* with benefits (free meals, entrance tickets and accommodation) in the beautiful town of Ohrid, Macedonia.

Applicants, please send a covering letter with your ²*work experience/ curriculum vitae (CV) or resumé* to the human resources manager. Click here for contact details.

Children's Recreation Supervisors

Are you outgoing, enthusiastic and ³*flexible/flexibility*? Do you love children? Global company Fun Parks are looking for kids' recreation supervisors for our new theme attraction, Pirate Park, opening soon at Lake Ohrid. ⁴*Group/Team* work and good language skills essential. Monthly salary: €775. On-the-job ⁵*training/supervision* provided.

Restaurant Managers

Do you have excellent communication and organizational ⁶*abilities/skills*? Do you work well under pressure? English-speaking Restaurant Manager needed for our nautical café at Pirate Park.

Diploma or degree in Food and beverages ⁷*managers/management* an advantage; minimum two years' ⁸*experience/working* required. Salary: €2,200 per month.

2 Work in pairs. Discuss which job in Exercise 1 you would prefer to do and why.

Listening

SKILLS AND QUALITIES

3))) **2.3** Listen to the human resources manager at Fun Parks. Which job does she talk about first?

4))) Listen again and make notes about the experience, skills and qualities needed for each job.

Reading

COVERING LETTERS

5 Read this covering letter from a job applicant. Which job is he applying for?

Dame Gruev, Gradski Blok 6, 1000 Skopje
Telephone: +389 23 116 074
Skype: Miroslav.Wasilew

Human Resources Manager
Fun Parks
Ref. 1179 Fun Park applications

Dear Ms Isabela Monti,

¹_____ for the position of Children's Recreation Supervisor ²_____ on your website on 15 October. I am very interested in working for Fun Parks because I enjoyed the Pirate Park very much when I visited it recently with a group of children.

At the moment, I am studying for a diploma in Tourism Management at the University of Macedonia in Skopje but I am looking for work during the summer vacation. I am in my first year, although ³_____ in working for an after-school club. ⁴_____ organizing activities and excursions for young children. Please ⁵_____.

My supervisor says I am outgoing, hard-working and creative. ⁶_____, I am enthusiastic and I work well in a team. ⁷_____ from my CV, I speak English and many Eastern European languages fluently.

If you are interested in my application, ⁸_____ regarding a possible interview. ⁹_____ hearing from you.

¹⁰_____

Miroslav Wasilew

---

6 Complete the letter in Exercise 5 with expressions from the Professional skills box.

7 Write a covering letter for the other job advertised in Exercise 1. Use the models in Exercise 5 and in the Writing bank on page 96 to help you. Include the information below.

- say why you want to work for the company
- mention any relevant qualifications and/or experience
- mention your main qualities and skills
- say you are interested in a job interview

Speaking

INTERVIEW QUESTIONS

8 **))) 2.4** Listen and write down ten job interview questions. What other typical questions can you ask?

9 Work in pairs. Take turns to read each other's covering letter from Exercise 7. Then take turns to interview each other for the job. Begin and end your interview like this:

> *Good morning/afternoon. Please take a seat.*
> *I'd like to ask you a few questions …*

> *OK, I'm afraid that's all we have time for today.*
> *Thank you for coming. We'll be in touch.*

PROFESSIONAL SKILLS:
WRITING A COVERING LETTER

I am writing to apply
As you can see
Yours sincerely,
In addition
find attached a copy of my CV
I have two years' experience
as advertised
My responsibilities include
please do not hesitate to contact me
I look forward to

CASE STUDY CHOOSE THE RIGHT PERSON FOR THE JOB

Aim: To choose the best candidate for the job of Assistant Cruise Director.

1 Read the job advertisement.
2 Complete the candidates' profiles.
3 Interview the candidates.
4 Meet to decide the best candidate.

Assistant Cruise Director

1 **Work in pairs. Read the job advert and make a list of the experience and personal qualities necessary to apply for the job.**

Assistant Cruise Director: salary $2,600–$2,800/month

We are looking for a motivated person for the post of Assistant Cruise Director.

Duties:
- meet and greet guests during embarkation and disembarkation
- help the cruise director in planning guest entertainment and in managing the entertainment budget
- *host daytime and evening activities, e.g. parties, game shows, bingo
- recruit, train and supervise entertainment staff
- socialize with guests and maintain a high level of passenger satisfaction

Requirements:
- strong organizational skills
- experience working with large groups of people and public speaking skills
- ability to interact with people of all ages
- minimum two years' experience in public relations, entertainment, recreation or guest services

Contract:
- six months on ship; six weeks' holiday
- return airfares, meals, accommodation and uniforms provided

*host = introduce a show

Candidate profiles

2 Read about two candidates for the job and complete their profiles. Do you think they are strong candidates?

1 Angelica Davies
   Age: 28
   Nationality: British
   Current position: ¹_____
   Personal qualities: ²_____
   Education and training: ³_____
   Experience and skills: ⁴_____

I started working on the front desk at a hotel when I was 18, and I learnt a lot about customer service skills there. I became a receptionist on a cruise ship five years ago. After two years, I moved into the Entertainment Department and I am now Shore Excursion Manager. I give presentations to passengers to promote and sell excursions before we arrive in each port. I also supervise the shore excursion staff. I think I have the right qualities for this job – I'm very outgoing, hard-working and flexible.

2 Bruno Rossi
   Age: 32
   Nationality: Italian
   Current position: ⁵_____
   Personal qualities: ⁶_____
   Education and training: ⁷_____
   Experience and skills: ⁸_____

I have sixteen years' experience as an entertainer. I left school at 15 and started work in a gift shop in Rimini. I learnt English talking to tourists in the shop. At weekends I play in a band. I became a singer, musician and DJ on cruise ships seven years ago. I often help the Cruise Director organize the entertainment and I host lots of activities. I'm extrovert and friendly and I enjoy entertaining people. I speak English, Italian and some Spanish, and I'm learning French at the moment.

3)))**2.5** Listen to the third candidate and complete her profile.

Julie Quinn
Age: 25
Nationality: Australian
Current position: Youth Activities Coordinator

Personal qualities: ¹_____
Education and training: ²_____
Experience and skills: ³_____

4 Work in pairs or small groups. Which candidate from Exercises 2 and 3 would you choose for the job and why?

TASK

5)))**2.6** Listen to part of the interview with Angelica Davies. Complete the questions 1–5 and make a note of Angelica's answers.

   1 Why do you ¹_____?

   2 What ²_____ do you ³_____?

   3 What do you ⁴_____ about working on a cruise ship? And what do you ⁵_____?

   4 What ideas do you have for ⁶_____?

   5 Why should we ⁷_____ this job?

6 Work in pairs. Student A turn to File 6, page 103. Student B turn to File 11, page 104. Roleplay the job interviews with Julie Quinn and Bruno Rossi.

7 Work in small groups. Discuss the best candidate for the job. Consider the following points:

   • personal qualities
   • education and training
   • experience and skills
   • interview performance

UNIT 2: KEY WORDS

communicative   deal with efficient   enthusiastic   flexible hard-working   outgoing qualification   recruit responsible for   seasonal   shift skills   temporary   training **See DVD-ROM Mini-dictionary**

3

VISITOR CENTRES

UNIT MENU

Grammar: comparative and superlative forms
Vocabulary: visitor information centres (VICs), adjectives
Professional skills: dealing with enquiries
Case study: improve a service

Listening

VISITOR INFORMATION AROUND THE WORLD

1))) 3.1 **Listen to two speakers. Which countries are they from?**

2))) **Listen again and correct the information in 1–6. Which information services are similar in your country?**

1 There are tourist offices in all the beach resorts in Spain.
2 They give advice on places to stay, eating out and things to see and do, e.g. sports events.
3 The Tourist Office usually gives the best information.
4 There are lots of VICs on the Chinese mainland.
5 Some Chinese VICs say they are 'official' organizations.
6 The Hong Kong and Macau tourism boards don't provide helpful advice.

Vocabulary

VICS

3 **Match the words 1–6 with the definitions a–f.**

1 sights	**a**	when you suggest or recommend what someone should do
2 attractions	**b**	thin book that gives information or advertises something
3 advice	**c**	piece of paper with information on it
4 event	**d**	popular places to visit or activities to do
5 leaflet	**e**	places that are interesting to see and that many people visit
6 brochure	**f**	something that is organized, e.g. a festival, sports game or show

4 **Look at the list of information and services that a VIC can provide. Think of THREE more things to add to the list.**

- leaflets and brochures for local sights and attractions, e.g. castles, theme parks
- emergency telephone numbers, e.g. police, hospital
- local opening hours/times and things to see and do, e.g. shopping, eating out

Reading

THE ROLE OF VICS

5 Read the article about the changing role of VICs and answer the questions.

1 Why do VICs not use the word 'tourist'?

2 Find two reasons why some people think VICs are not necessary.

3 Find two reasons why VICs are still useful.

The changing role of VICs

These days, many Tourist Information Centres (TICs) in the UK have changed their name to *Visitor Information Centres* or VICs. After research by the Scottish Tourist Board showed that 50 percent of visitors to TICs were Scottish and not 'tourists', TICs began to change. They started diversifying their services and designing publicity material not just for traditional tourists but for all kinds of visitors to the area.

Not everyone thinks that this is a good thing. Some hoteliers, for example, think that VICs are unnecessary because most travel purchases are made *before* arrival. Visitors can get information from hotel receptions, taxi drivers or shop assistants. Visitors can also get online information 24/7 using laptops or mobile devices in hotels with Wi-Fi connections. Many VICs now have information technology and interactive computer screens. Although the centres provide a useful service it costs a lot of public money to run them, which some believe could be used to promote the region in other ways.

However, other tourism professionals believe that VICs are an effective way of promoting both regional and national tourism. They give *free* information to *all* visitors including hotel guests, local residents and day-trippers. VICs encourage visitors to see more and do more: visiting local sights and attractions, and going to festivals or sports events. Many visitors prefer face-to-face contact with professionals who can help find accommodation, give them advice during their stay, sell maps and guides, and most importantly, are ambassadors for the area.

6 Read the article in Exercise 5 again and complete sentences 1–6 with words from the text. The first letter of each word is given to help you.

1 Visitor Information Centres, or [1]V _____ are sometimes called [2]T _____ Information Centres (TICs).

2 The function of a VIC is to [3]p _____ the local area by giving free information and [4]a _____.

3 Many visitor centres today have digital tourist information and advanced information [5]t _____.

4 The role of VICs is to make sure visitors see the main [6]s _____ and attractions or go to local [7]e _____.

5 Many visitors value the [8]f _____ contact in a VIC and enjoy talking to a local person.

6 Visitor Information Officers have to deal with all kinds of [9]e _____, and have an important role as [10]a _____ for the region.

Speaking

LOCAL INFORMATION

7 Discuss the questions below with a partner.

1 What are the main attractions in your local area? List five in order of importance (1 = the most important).

2 What do tourists find surprising about your region, e.g. opening hours/times?

> ### RESEARCH
>
> **YOUR LOCAL AREA**
> Visit the website of your local VIC and find a map of your area. Find out the opening times, information about the main attractions, places to eat and details about any special events this week.

BHUTAN

Reading

BHUTAN – THE HAPPIEST COUNTRY IN THE WORLD

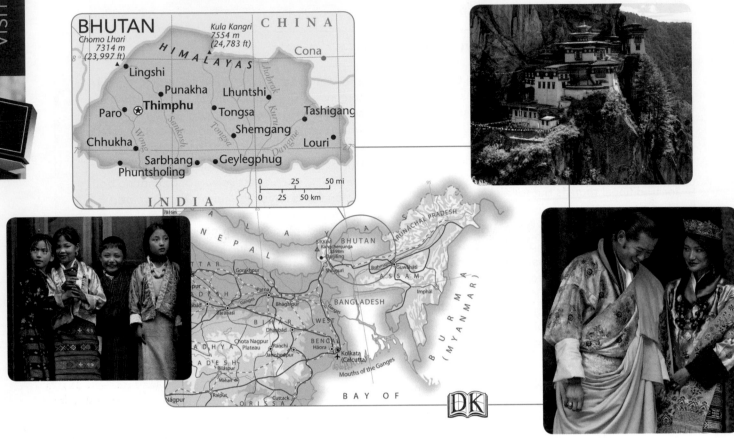

1 What do you know about Bhutan? Compare your ideas with a partner.

2 Read the article and match the sentence halves 1–4 with a–d to make true statements about Bhutan.

Bhutan – the happiest country in the world

The tiny kingdom of Bhutan is a country in a remote part of the Himalayas. The country has a rich heritage and is full of spectacular monasteries called *Dzongs* – which is also the origin of the name for the Bhutanese language, *dzongkha*.

Although Bhutan may not be one of the richest countries in the world, it is officially one of the happiest. The government of Bhutan believes in promoting the nation's 'gross national happiness' (GNH). The King first used the phrase GNH in 1972 and his son, one of the world's youngest heads of states, rules with the same philosophy.

Bhutan is an isolated country and its airport, Paro, is one of the most spectacular but also one of the scariest airports in the world to land in. The route through the mountains is very difficult to navigate and only ten pilots know how to! The Tourism Council of Bhutan is training cooks and guides in cultural and trek tourism, both of which are popular. However, the government wants to prevent mass tourism so visitors have to pay a tourism tax of $165 to $200 per day.

1 Only the most experienced pilots	a people in the world.
2 Today Bhutan is not as isolated	b of GNH.
3 The Bhutanese are some of the happiest	c can land at Bhutan's airport.
4 The former king invented the idea	d as it was before.

3 Would you like to live and work in Bhutan? Why/Why not?

GRAMMAR: COMPARATIVE AND SUPERLATIVE FORMS

Comparative forms

1 Add **-er** to adjectives, e.g. *younger, richer* than.
Note: spelling change for adjectives ending in **y**, e.g. *happier, scarier, easier* than.
Double the final letter for adjectives ending consonant-vowel-consonant, e.g. *bigger, thinner, sadder* than.

2 Add **more** to adjectives of two syllables or more, e.g. **more** *modern*, **more** *isolated* than.

Superlative forms

1 Use **the** and add **-est** to adjectives, e.g. **the** *youngest, richest, biggest*.
Note: spelling change for adjectives that end in **y**, e.g. *the happiest, the friendliest*.

2 Add **the most** to adjectives of two syllables or more, e.g. **the most** *modern*, **the most** *spectacular*.

Irregular forms

good → better → best
bad → worse → worst

See Grammar reference, page 113.

4 Study the Grammar box and <u>underline</u> examples of superlative forms in the article in Exercise 2.

5 Read about changes in modern Bhutan. Complete the text with the adjectives in the box.

> best   bigger   friendlier   happiest   important   longer   modern   traditional

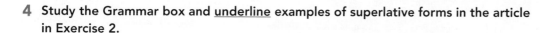

Things are changing for Bhutan. Bhutan today has newer roads than before. Television only arrived in 1999. You can see more ¹_____ and more Western influences in Thimpu, although the capital has no traffic lights. The city prefers to employ policemen – traffic police are ²_____ than traffic lights.
The Bhutanese think the most ³_____ things in life are happiness, the environment, health, education and community spirit. Bhutan's culture is unique and it wants to develop its tourism differently from its ⁴_____ neighbours.
Another way of preserving Bhutan's culture is by having a more ⁵_____ dress code. Men wear a long robe and women wear the kira, a ⁶_____ dress. If you're travelling to one of the ⁷_____ places in the world, make sure you pack long black socks, lip gloss and tea. They make the ⁸_____ presents for Bhutanese people.

6 Complete the sentences with the words in brackets in the correct form. You will need ONE or TWO words.

1 Bhutan is _____ (modern) than it was ten years ago.

2 Bhutan's airport has some of the _____ (spectacular) views in the world.

3 The Bhutanese government says its people are _____ (happy) other nationalities.

4 The nightlife in Thimpu isn't as _____ (good) the nightlife in Beijing or Delhi.

5 The Bhutanese eat lots of chilli. Their food is _____ (spicy) the food in China.

6 The disco in Thimpu is _____ (noisy) the karaoke pool hall.

7 Bhutanese men wear a _____ (short) robe _____ the women.

8 Bhutan is one of _____ (tiny) countries in the world.

7 **Compare your country with Bhutan. Write at least SIX sentences using comparative forms. Compare your ideas with a partner.**

e.g. *The air in Bhutan is cleaner than in my country.*

RESEARCH

COMPARING COUNTRIES
Find information on two countries you don't know very well. Compare them and present your findings.

Speaking

THE BEST AND THE WORST

8 **Work in pairs. Make a list of the best and worst aspects of your country. Use the words and phrases in the box. Then compare your ideas with another pair.**

> climate   clothes   food   landscape   location   nightlife
> people   tourism industry   traditions   transport

PROFESSIONAL SKILLS
DEALING WITH ENQUIRIES

Listening

TYPICAL ENQUIRIES

1 What do you know about the attractions in Edinburgh?

2))) 3.2 Listen to the manager of Edinburgh's VisitScotland Information Centre talking about the work of the centre. Complete the information.

    1 The VisitScotland Information Centre gets [1]_____ of enquiries every [2]_____.

    2 Tourists typically want [3]_____ and information about the city's attractions.

    3 The Edinburgh Pass provides [4]_____ on attractions, bus tours and transport.

Reading

EDINBURGH BUS TOURS

3 Read the article. Are the statements true (T) or false (F)? Correct the false statements.

    1 Passengers can get on and off the bus at any stop on the route. T / F

    2 There is recorded commentary in nine languages. T / F

    3 The bus tour does not operate at night. T / F

    4 There is entertainment for children. T / F

Edinburgh Bus Tours – History on the move

The best way to find out about Edinburgh's inspiring history. With over 500,000 passengers every year, Edinburgh Bus Tours is Scotland's second most visited paid attraction.

Each tour, with live commentary in English, offers a great introduction to Scotland's capital city. What's more, our hop-on, hop-off tickets give you the flexibility to visit the famous sights around the city as we pass them.

- Commentary through headphones in French, German, Spanish, Italian, Dutch, Russian, Mandarin Chinese and Japanese
- 24-hour ticket
- HORRIBLE HISTORY English language channel for kids (and grown-ups too!)
- Hop-on, hop-off to visit the sights
- Main sights: New Town, St Andrew Square, Old Town, Edinburgh Castle, National Museum of Scotland, Scottish Parliament, Our Dynamic Earth

Listening

TELEPHONE ENQUIRIES

4))) 3.3 Listen to an assistant at Edinburgh's VIC dealing with a telephone enquiry and complete the adverts. Which tour does the caller want?

City sightseeing bus tour

- Leave from Waverley Bridge every [1]_____
- Tickets valid on all tour buses [2]_____
- Full itinerary takes [3]_____
- Tickets cost [4]£_____ for adults, £13 for seniors/students and £6 for children under 16

Guided walking tours of the old town

- Starting from the Tourist Information Centre
- Duration of tour: [5]_____ minutes
- Start times: 10 a.m., [6]_____, 2.30 p.m. and 4.30 p.m. every day in summer
- Cost: [7]£_____ for adults, and [8]_____ for children under eight and senior citizens

5 Complete the expressions in the Professional skills box. Use ONE to THREE words in each gap. Look at audio script 3.3 on page 120 and check your answers.

PROFESSIONAL SKILLS: DEALING WITH ENQUIRIES

Starting the call
Hello, VisitScotland Information Centre. Paula speaking. [1]_____ help you?

Checking and confirming
Sorry, [2]_____ the guided tours or the bus tours?
Would you like to book the tour?
Just let me check/confirm those details.

Active listening
[3]_____. There are four bus tours.
Right. You can buy the tickets from the driver.
I see. Which is the best tour?

Promising action
I'll book that for you.
I'll hold your reservation until 2 p.m.

Finishing the call
Can I do anything else for you?
You're [4]_____. Would you like anything else?
Thank you [5]_____ the centre.

Vocabulary

NUMBERS IN ENQUIRIES

6 Match the questions 1–5 with the answers a–e. Practise saying the numbers and phrases.

1 How much is the Edinburgh Pass?

2 How long is the bus tour?

3 What time does the ghost tour start?

4 Can retired people get cheaper tickets for festival events?

5 What's the discount for children?

a Tours depart daily at 9.30 p.m. and 10.15 p.m., and last an hour and fifteen minutes.

b Yes, senior citizens and full-time students are eligible for concession-priced tickets.

c A one-day adult pass costs £29, and a two-day pass is £39.

d The full itinerary is 90 minutes.

e Admission is £6 for children under 16, and free of charge to children under three.

Speaking

DEALING WITH ENQUIRIES

7 Work in pairs. Roleplay the situations. Student A turn to File 8, page 103. Student B turn to File 10, page 104.

CASE STUDY
IMPROVE A SERVICE

CASE STUDY MENU

Aim: To analyse and improve the customer service at a VIC.

1 Listen to a mystery shopper's report and make notes.
2 Read and analyse feedback from customers.
3 Read reports about the website and the visitors' survey.
4 Decide priorities for improving the service.

Mystery shopper

1 Work in pairs. Read the text and answer the questions.

1 What do you think are the advantages and disadvantages of using a mystery shopper to collect information about the quality of a service?

2 What other ways are there to investigate the quality of a service?

What is a mystery shopper?

Many organizations use 'mystery' consumers or shoppers to collect information and check the quality of their services. These mystery shoppers act as normal customers and perform specific tasks, e.g. ask questions or buy a product. Then, they give detailed reports or feedback about their experiences.

Albertville Visitors Bureau

2))) 3.4 Albertville Visitors Bureau in Canada investigates the quality of all its visitor centres. Listen to one mystery shopper's feedback and make notes about the following for each centre.

a response to email and telephone enquiries

b staff welcome

c appearance

Customer feedback

3 Read the customer feedback A and B on the next page and answer the questions.

1 What problem(s) does each person identify with the service?

2 What action(s) could the Bureau take in response to these comments?

A I visited your centre with my husband who is in a wheelchair. There are steps outside the building and no ramp so he could not come into the building. Also, I think the door is narrow and a wheelchair could not pass through it. I think it's very important that a public service is adapted for people with special needs like my husband.

B I don't understand why you close your centres at lunchtime and on Sundays, especially in the summer. A lot of visitors to your town are only there for a few days or the weekend and can't get the information they need. And the opening hours are not on the outside of the building, which is very frustrating. I had to go to your website to find this information.

Website evaluation

4 The Albertville Visitors Bureau asked a consultant to evaluate its website. Read the report. Which options do you think are a good idea and why?

Website evaluation: Albertville Visitors Bureau

Visitor centres in Albertville are experiencing a decline in the number of visitors. At the same time, more and more people are turning to our website and other online guides to access tourist information services.

This is a clear indication that a lot of visitors are doing their own research and bookings using the internet, and that the region needs to improve the services we offer on the website.

Options to consider are:
1 provide an online accommodation booking service
2 add printable PDF versions of maps and information to the website
3 produce videos with virtual tours on the website
4 have interactive user forums for feedback and suggestions
5 open digital tourist kiosks in key locations
6 close one of the visitor centres to cover the cost of improvements to the website

TASK

5 Work in pairs or small groups. You are managers at the Albertville Visitors Bureau. Read the report from a visitor survey in File 12 on page 104. Consider this with the other information you have collected and hold a meeting.

1 Compile a list of the main strengths and weaknesses of the Bureau's service.

2 Discuss what aspects you most need to improve, and complete the table.

3 Decide your top three priorities.

4 Present your decisions to the class.

	Low cost	High cost
Essential improvements		
Desirable improvements		

Formal email

6 Write a formal email to the mayor and local government of Albertville explaining how you plan to improve the Visitors Bureau.

UNIT 3: KEY WORDS

advice   attraction   brochure
discount   event   feedback
improve   leaflet   provide
recommend   remote   sights
sightseeing   unique   wheelchair
See DVD-ROM Mini-dictionary

4

PACKAGE TOURS

UNIT MENU

Grammar: past simple
Vocabulary: cultural heritage, packages
Professional skills: city tours
Case study: design a package

Vocabulary

CULTURAL HERITAGE

1 <u>Underline</u> the odd word in each group. Explain your choice. Use a dictionary to help you.

1 parliament / courts of justice / prime minister's residence / city hall / square

2 science museum / big wheel / concert hall / art gallery / wax model museum

3 palace / mansion / theatre / country house / castle

4 pillar / façade / dome / bridge / roof

5 wooden / stone / Baroque / iron / glass

6 Roman / Medieval / Renaissance / the sixties / Post-modern

Reading

THINGS YOU DIDN'T KNOW ABOUT LONDON

2 Work in pairs. Read some historical facts about London. Then cover the facts. How many do you remember?

Did you know ...?

1 The Roman city of Londinium had a busy port and soon developed into a capital city.

2 The first stone bridge over the River Thames was built in 1209 and lasted 600 years.

3 In the Middle Ages, sanitary conditions weren't good and many Londoners died of the plague in 1349.

4 The Great Fire of 1666 started in a bakery and burnt for three days. Most buildings didn't survive, except for The Tower of London and Westminster Abbey.

5 One million people lived in London at the start of the 19th century. It was one of the largest cities in the world at the time.

GRAMMAR: PAST SIMPLE

Regular verbs

1 Add **-ed** or **-d** to regular verbs.
*London's first stone bridge last**ed** 600 years.*
*Many Londoners die**d** of the plague in 1349.*

2 Use **didn't** + **infinitive** for negative forms.
*Most buildings **didn't survive** the Great Fire of London.*

Use **did** + **subject** + **infinitive** for question forms.
***Did you know** that the smell from the Thames was very bad?*

Past passive

Use **was**/**were** + the past participle
*The building **was designed** by Wren.*
*The first bridge **was built** in 1209.*

Irregular verbs

Many common verbs have an irregular form – see page 117 for a list.
*Henry VIII **had** six wives.*
The Great Fire burnt for three days.

Past of be

Use **was/were**, or **wasn't/weren't** for the negative.
*It **was** the largest city in Europe.*
*Sanitary conditions **weren't** good.*

See Grammar reference, pages 113 and 114.

3 Study the Grammar box. <u>Underline</u> the verbs in the past simple tense in the historical facts in Exercise 2.

4 Complete the article with the correct past simple form of the verbs in brackets.

Historic London

Hampton Court in Richmond, London ¹_____ (be/not) originally a royal palace. It ²_____ (be) Cardinal Wolsey's country house but Wolsey then ³_____ (give) it to King Henry VIII in 1528. Later Hampton Court was ⁴_____ (rebuild) by the architect, Christopher Wren, so its architectural style is a mix of Tudor and English Baroque. Hampton Court is famous for the maze in its gardens and the indoor royal tennis court. People say tennis ⁵_____ (invent) by Henry VIII.

The British Museum first ⁶_____ (open) in 1753 and is the oldest public museum in the world. The museum covers 4 km and has Greek, Roman and Egyptian collections. Famous figures like Karl Marx and Mahatma Gandhi once ⁷_____ (read) in the Reading Room. In 1845, a visitor ⁸_____ (break) one of the exhibits, the Portland vase, into 200 pieces. The vase ⁹_____ (be) over 2,000 years old but the museum ¹⁰_____ (put) it together again.

Vocabulary

SAYING YEARS

Before 2000, say the year in two figures, e.g. 1349 (*thirteen forty-nine*), 1906 (*nineteen oh six*)
Say 2000–2009 as one number, e.g. 2004 (*two thousand and four*).
After 2010, you can say the year in two figures or as one number, e.g. 2012 (*two thousand and twelve* or *twenty twelve*).

5 **))) 4.1** Read the text about saying years. Then listen and write down the years and dates you hear.

e.g. 1 *1666*

6 Write down THREE important dates in your country's history. Present your ideas to the class.

Speaking

A TWO-HOUR TOUR

7 When was the last time you went on a tour? What was the tour guide like? What were the good and bad things about the tour? Compare your ideas with a partner.

8 Work in pairs. Turn to File 13 on page 104.

RESEARCH

LANDMARK BUILDINGS
Choose three important landmark buildings in your capital city and answer the questions.
1 When were they built?
2 Who were the architects?
3 What are the architectural styles and main features?

CANCÚN

Reading

RESORT DEVELOPMENT IN CANCÚN

1 Look at the map and photos of Cancún below. Which features of the island do you think make it attractive to tourists?

2 Read the text about tourist development in Cancún and answer the questions.

1 What was Cancún like before 1970? **2** What is it like now?

Cancún – Mexico's leading destination

Mexico's mass tourism industry is dominated by large-scale, purpose-built developments. In 1967, responding to the USA's demand for beach vacations, Mexico's central bank identified the five best places for new, purpose-built tourist resorts. Top of the list, as part of a 30-year plan, was a sandy island, now known as Cancún.

Before 1970, Cancún was a small fishing village of about 100 inhabitants. Cancún is now Mexico's leading tourist resort. When the National Tourism Development Fund, Fonatur, began building Cancún in 1970 they considered these factors: warm water temperatures, sandy beaches, varied attractions, sunshine hours and travel distances from the main markets. The benefits were thousands of new jobs, the development of a region and growth of the Mexican economy.

Public funds were used to buy land and install necessary basic infrastructure: an airport, highways, drinking water, electricity, telephone lines, a convention center, golf course and harbors. Private investors also developed hotels, a shopping mall and other services.

The increase in the number of visitors to Cancún was dramatic. In 1975, Cancún had 1,769 hotel rooms in service. By 2008, there were about 150 hotels and more than 27,000 rooms. Cancún airport now handles 200 flights a day. Cancún's population went up from 30,000 in 1980 to about 600,000 today. Cancún is now only one part of an extensive tourist region along the Quintana Roo coast, on what is known today as the Mayan Riviera.

3 Read the text in Exercise 2 again and write what each number below refers to.

a 5 _____	**d** 1,000s _____	**g** 200 _____
b 30 _____	**e** 1,769 _____	**h** 600,000 _____
c 100 _____	**f** 150 _____	

4 Look at the list of basic infrastructure that a tourism resort needs in paragraph 3 of the text in Exercise 2. Can you think of any other necessary basic infrastructure?

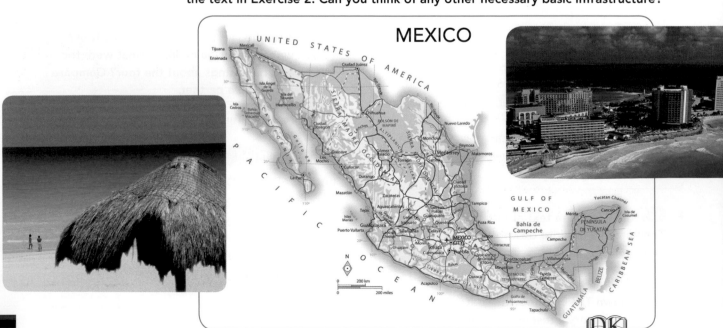

MEXICO

Vocabulary

PACKAGES

5 Work in pairs. Which items in the box are usually included in a package tour to a beach resort? Which items are optional extras?

> airport transfers   babysitters   beach umbrellas   car/boat hire
> evening entertainment   flights   free activities for kids   free drinks   gratuity
> hire of sports equipment   information pack   meals   sightseeing tours

6 <u>Underline</u> the word in 1–6 that you CAN'T use with the noun on the right.

1 sandy, harbour, quiet, city	beach
2 clear, drinking, fish, warm	water
3 growth, evening, children's, free	entertainment
4 low, warm, clear, high	temperatures
5 tourist, sandy, large, purpose-built	resort
6 tropical, desert, uninhabited, coast	island

7 Read the sentences about a package tour and circle the best word or expression in italics.

1 Our *all-inclusive / all together / all-in-one* package includes the cost of travel, transfers, hotel, meals, and some activities and tours.

2 You stay *half-board / full-board / for free* – all meals are included.

3 If you need specific services during your stay you can book a(n) *tailored / all-inclusive / cheap* package.

4 Our private beaches are exclusive to the resort and are never *crowded / sandy / quiet* with day trippers.

5 For families with small children, a(n) *babysitting / entertainment / tour guide* service is available at a small extra cost.

6 The hotel offers free *extras / entertainment / beverages* in the evenings with music.

7 You need to *sign / signature / sign up* in advance if you want to come on the boat trip to the island tomorrow.

8 Gratuities are included in all-inclusive deals but guests sometimes tip staff and *pay extra / overcharge / pay back* when they want a quality service.

Valerie Schroder

Listening

PACKAGE TOURS TO CANCÚN

8))) **4.2** Listen to Valerie Schroder (1) and Jason Alvarez (2) talking about their holidays in Cancún. Who …

a was on their honeymoon? ___

b was disappointed by the beach? ___

c found some things expensive and commercial? ___

d wants to go back to Mexico? ___

9))) Listen again and answer the questions.

1 What was included in Valerie's package tour to Cancún?

2 What was included in Jason's package tour to Cancún?

10 Work in pairs. What kind of package do you prefer: an all-inclusive or a tailored package? Why? What are the advantages and disadvantages of these packages?

Jason Alvarez

PROFESSIONAL SKILLS
CITY TOURS

Listening

BARCELONA CITY TOURS

1 What do you know about Barcelona? What attractions could you include on a city tour? Compare your ideas with a partner.

2 Read about the Barcelona tours. Match the tours 1–3 to the items a–f. Which tour would you like to go on?

a a free show ____

b visits to religious buildings ____

c shopping ____

d a quiz ____

e a UNESCO World Heritage site ____

f visit to an art museum ____

Barcelona tours

Our tour guides are experienced, informative and fun! Tailored tours for large groups available.

1 Gothic history tour: Visit Barcelona's old town and see the beautiful Gothic basilica of Santa Maria del Mar. Complete the tour with tapas in one of Barcelona's stylish cafés. This tour lasts two hours and includes a history quiz!

2 Gaudí tour: This architectural tour includes buildings designed by the well-known Catalan architect with free time for checking out Barcelona's designer stores. Then take a relaxing walk in Gaudí's fabulous park, Parc Guell, a UNESCO

World Heritage site. Four-hour tour including a €5.00 shopping voucher!

3 Montjuic tour: See the Best Romanesque art museum in Europe and enjoy modern works of art at the Miró Foundation. Take advantage of spectacular views of Barcelona from Montjuic hill. Enjoy an optional dinner at a theme 'village' with replicas of Spain's most famous buildings or go shopping in the former bullring. The evening ends with a free music and light show at the Magic Fountains. One-day tour.

---

3))) **4.3** Listen to a Barcelona tour and answer the questions.

1 Which tour is it?

2 What are the four places that are mentioned?

3 What can't the woman find?

4))) Listen again and complete the sentences and questions 1–6.

1 Here we are! As you _____, the former bullring was made into a shopping centre not very long ago.

2 Plaza Arenas is now _____ Arenas.

3 That's a _____. The British architect, Richard Rogers, renovated it.

4 Would you like to _____ now into the art gallery?

5 Right, _____ and see their collection of Romanesque Art.

6 _____ your art tickets please?

5))) **4.4** Listen to another tour and answer the questions.

1 Which tour is it?

2 What kind(s) of questions do the visitors ask?

3 When was the basilica completed?

6))) Read the sentences. Listen again and circle the option(s) in italics you hear.

1 [1]*Can / Is it OK if* I take a few photos?

2 Sure, [2]*go ahead / no problem* but no flash please.

3 It only took [3]*45 / 55* years to build, which was [4]*very slow / incredibly fast* for Medieval times.

4 The windows date from the [5]*15th to 18th / 16th to 19th* centuries.

5 [6]*Excuse me / Hey*, where is the [7]*toilet / restroom*?

6 Here. [8]*Mind / Be careful of* the step as you go.

7 Complete the Professional skills with the expressions in the box.

> 3–9 days   all meals   extra charge   Friday evening   major cities
> printed information   short tour   short visits and all-day
> specialist knowledge   special needs

PROFESSIONAL SKILLS: PLANNING CITY TOURS

1 Offer tours to _____ like London, Paris or Rome.

2 Design city *package tours for _____ .

3 Find out if participants have any _____ beforehand, e.g. problems with mobility.

4 Start the tour on a _____ to make the most of weekend activities.

5 Offer an additional _____ in a nearby city either before or after the main tour.

6 Don't include _____ . Some people don't want to always eat with the group.

7 Include both _____ excursions, sightseeing, some meals and social activities. But leave some free time.

8 Make sure participants know the full cost and which activities have an _____ .

9 Use local tour guides for _____ .

10 Give out maps and _____ .

*package tour = American English, package holiday = British English

---

8 The Professional skills 1–10 in Exercise 7 are for designing tours for American tourists. Which skills would work well for people from your country and which would be different? Why? Compare your ideas with a partner.

Speaking

PROPOSING A WORLD HERITAGE SITE

9 Work in pairs or groups of four. Student A turn to File 7, page 103. Student B turn to File 15, page 105.

CASE STUDY
DESIGN A PACKAGE

Aim: To redesign a one-week musical package tour.

1 Read about an Austrian tour company and its musical package tours.
2 Listen to feedback on tour products from customers and employees.
3 Read about and analyse a competitors' tour package in Austria.
4 Plan a more competitive package tour.

Capital city	Vienna, home of the Viennese waltz
Population	over eight million
Geographical features	Austrian Alps with high peaks, mountain grasslands
Austrian composers	Mozart, Haydn, Schubert, Johann, Strauss (son), Mahler

Europa Cultural Tours

1 **Read about the tours offered by Austrian tour operator Europa Cultural Tours (ECT). The company was successful in the past but is now losing money. Why do you think this is? Compare your ideas with a partner. Think about …**

1 Organization: length of tours, activities and tour guides.

2 Products: classical or too commercial?

3 Price: too high/low?

4 Target market: seniors/ families/couples/singles?

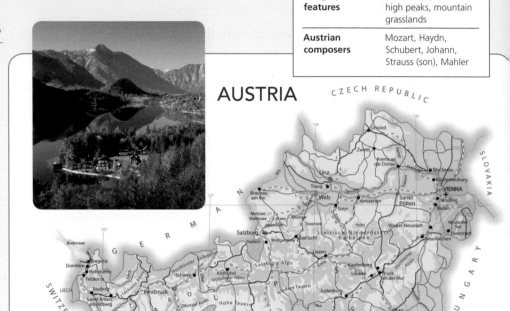

AUSTRIA

Europa Cultural Tours

The Danube Festival: A festival of music and poetry and an opportunity to hear international singers and pianists in six days! We offer private concerts on this all-inclusive package: flights, accommodation, meals and concert tickets included. Choice of hotel accommodation or cruise. Enjoy Austrian scenery from the comfort of a river cruise, with 12 concerts at the Mozarteum concert hall! Or do the walking tour, staying in four-star hotels, walking in the morning and attending six concerts in the afternoons.
Price: €3,810 pp cabin for two, €4,600 pp single cabin; walking tour – €1,630 pp. Suitable for couples, singles and senior citizens (under 75).

Salzburg summer festival: Enjoy three operas and three concerts at the world's best music festival in five days. This cultural tour includes music talks and excursions in the charming city of Salzburg – see the best art, architecture and scenery in Austria! Can be booked on its own or together with The Danube Festival.
Price: €3,980 pp. Luxury hotel with river views. Package includes flights to Munich from major cities.

Feedback from customers and employees

2))) **4.5**   **Listen to two customers and an employee from ECT. What are their criticisms of the package tours? Listen again and tick (✓) your recommendations.**

1 ___ offer more classical tours

2 ___ employ more experienced guides

3 ___ leave more time for senior citizens to rest

4 ___ increase the amount of walking

5 ___ book more expensive accommodation

6 ___ be more transparent about extra costs

7 ___ give guides more training

8 ___ include more time for shopping

9 ___ lower prices

10 ___ offer tours for younger people

The competition

3 **Work in pairs. Read about the two most popular tours that ECT's competitor, Melody Tours, has on offer. Compare your information and answer the questions. Student A look at the tour information below. Student B look at the tour information in File 33, page 110.**

1 Which company offers the most expensive tour(s)?

2 Which company offers tours of film locations?

3 Which tour offers the best value for money?

4 What kind of people do you think book with ECT?

5 What kind of people do you think book with Melody Tours? Why do you think they are successful?

Sound of Music Bus Tour

Come to our charming city of Salzburg where Mozart was born and where the film *The Sound of Music* was made in 1965. Over five days our friendly guide, Andreas, and driver, Stefanie, show you the film locations: the convent where the film starts, Mirabell Gardens, Leopoldskron Palace, the residence of the Von Trapp family, the romantic Hellbrunn Palace and many more locations! Highlight of the tour is the building of the wedding scene in the picturesque village of Mondsee. Listen to the songs of the film at our musical theatre dinner. Fun for singles, couples and all the family!
Optional musical theatre dinner: €60, children half-price!
Accommodation: five nights, three-star hotel; single, double or family rooms available, breakfast included
Price: €750/€950/€1,150 depending on room type

The Sound of Music was a popular Hollywood musical film based on the story of the Von Trapp family.

TASK

4 **Work in pairs or small groups. Design a NEW competitive five-day musical package tour in Austria for ECT. Decide who the tour is for and how you will advertise it. Give your tour a name and include these points:**

1 accommodation (type and price)

2 travel and all transfers

3 concerts (how many and when?)

4 excursions (include one short tour and an all-day tour)

5 information about tour guides

6 social activities

7 an optional post-tour in Austria

8 total cost

5 **Present your tour to the class.**

UNIT 4: KEY WORDS

all-inclusive architecture art
babysitter building
entertainment gratuity
harbour historic island
lounger resort
sandy snorkelling tailored
transfers tropical
See DVD-ROM Mini-dictionary

5

HOTELS

UNIT MENU

Grammar: modal verbs
Vocabulary: hotel services and facilities, hotel trends, hotel charges
Professional skills: dealing with complaints
Case study: make a good hotel great

Reading

HOTELS IN MOSCOW

1 Read the guidebook extract about accommodation in Moscow. Are the tourists' comments 1–4 correct or incorrect?

1 'I'm sure there are lots of hotels in the city.'

2 'I expect the service isn't as good as in luxury hotels in the USA.'

3 'It'll be easy to find a cheap hotel in the city centre.'

4 'I hear it's a good idea to book a hotel before you get there.'

Accommodation in Moscow

Despite expansion, there are still not enough hotels in the Russian capital to meet demand. The foreign visitor is, in effect, limited to hotels in three categories: luxury hotels, the newer mid-price hotels and the cheaper, more basic ex-Soviet hotels. Most luxury hotels are in the centre and offer a similar service to the best hotels in the West. However, a double room costs the equivalent of $300 per night or more.

There aren't many mid-price hotels and there are very few budget hotels that cost less than $100 per night. Many of the cheaper hotels and the ex-Soviet hotels are located far from the centre.

It is best to reserve a room before arriving in Moscow. Hotels are often booked up months in advance, especially during the summer season. Visitors can get cheaper rates if they book with a travel agent or online, rather than reserve directly with a hotel.

Listening

CHECK-IN PROCEDURES

2  **Look at the check-in stages 1–7 for the Petrovskaya Hotel in Moscow. Then listen and write what the receptionist says at each stage.**

1 Smile and greet the guest.

2 Ask for the guest's passport or photo ID. Check their reservation on the computer.

3 Address the guest by name. Confirm the reservation details.

4 Ask the guest for a credit card as a deposit on the room.

5 Give the key card to the guest, say what floor the room is on and show them the room number.

6 Ask if the guest needs assistance with luggage.

7 Wish the guest an enjoyable stay.

3 **Why do you think the receptionist doesn't say the room number? Look at audio script 5.1 on page 121 and roleplay the conversation with a partner.**

4 🔊 **5.2** **Listen to a couple checking into the Petrovskaya Hotel. Complete the reservation details. What does the receptionist try to sell the guests?**

> **Guest name(s):** Mr and Mrs D. Golubkov
> **Room type:** ¹_____
>
> **Number of nights:** ²_____
> **Breakfast included:** ³*Yes / No*

GRAMMAR: MODAL VERBS

Use a **modal verb** with a main verb to form a sentence or a question.

Use the modal verbs **may**, **could** and **can** in questions to make requests.

Can I/Could I/May I see your passport and visa?

Could and *may* sound more polite in requests than *can*.

Use the modal verb **shall** in questions to make offers.

Shall I call the porter?

See Grammar reference, page 114.

5 **What would the hotel staff say in the situations below? Study the Grammar box and make requests or offers using the words in brackets and appropriate modal verbs.**

1 A guest asks reception to confirm her flight home by phone. (show me flight details)

e.g. *Could I have your flight details, please?*

2 A guest is paying for room service. (need credit card and guest to sign)

3 A guest is checking out and needs to go to the airport. (order a taxi?)

4 A guest orders drinks in the hotel café. (charge to guest room/room number?)

5 A guest wants to eat in the hotel restaurant this evening. (reserve a table?)

6 A guest wants to check out. (need key card and room number)

Speaking

CHECKING IN GUESTS

6 **Work in pairs. Student A look at the information below. Roleplay the check-in situations with Student B. Use the check-in stages 1–7 in Exercise 2. Student B turn to File 16, page 105.**

Student A: check-in 1
- You are a receptionist at the Petrovskaya Hotel.
- Confirm that the guest's reservation is a double room for three nights.
- Breakfast is included in the reservation. Breakfast time is from 7.30 a.m. to 9.30 a.m. in the ground floor restaurant.
- The guest's room is on the fifth floor.

Student A: check-in 2
- You are a guest checking into the Victoria Hotel.
- Your name is Nabil Miladi.
- You reserved a junior suite for six nights.
- You want to have dinner in the hotel restaurant tonight.

ROOM WITH A VIEW

Vocabulary

HOTEL SERVICES AND FACILITIES

1 **Which words in the box are hotel services and facilities? Which are guest room facilities?**

> 24-hour front desk   cot/crib   express checkout kiosk   fitness centre   hairdryer
> indoor swimming pool   in-room safe   iron   laundry service   walk-in shower

2 **Match the words in the box with the pictures.**

> blanket   duvet   hand lotion   pillow   shampoo   sheet   shower gel   soap

Toiletries:

  1 _____
  2 _____
  3 _____
  4 _____

Bedclothes:

  5 _____
  6 _____
  7 _____
  8 _____

Listening

GUEST EXPECTATIONS

3 **))) 5.3** **Listen to Kelly talking about what she wants from a hotel when she is travelling on business. Tick (✓) the facilities that are important. What other facilities or services does she mention?**

1 ___ high-speed internet access

2 ___ secretarial support

3 ___ work desk

4 ___ voicemail

5 ___ meeting room

6 ___ computer

7 ___ business centre

8 ___ printer

9 ___ colour photocopier

10 ___ technical support

4 **))) 5.4** **Listen to Kelly talking about what she wants from a hotel when she is travelling on holiday. Are the statements true (T) or false (F)? Correct the false statements.**

1 She goes on holiday with her husband and two children. T / F

2 She shares a room with her children. T / F

3 Children's entertainment at the hotel is important. T / F

4 She never uses the babysitting service. T / F

Reading

TRENDS IN THE HOTEL INDUSTRY

5 **Read the article on the next page and complete it with the correct paragraph headings in the box.**

> Changing demographics   Guest room technology
> My stay, my preferences   No extra costs

Trends in the hotel industry

1 _____

The hotel industry is adapting to new types of guests. Many hotels in the USA and Europe are changing their menus for international visitors from emerging markets, and employing Chinese-speaking staff. Guest room design is changing to meet the needs of older and richer travellers. Lower beds, brighter lighting and walk-in showers are easier to use and, at the same time, attractive to younger consumers.

2 _____

Hotels are changing their online reservations systems to allow guests to **choose** more elements of their stay. Guests can choose the room type, request a king-size bed or a sea view, **book** a romantic dinner on the first night or a spa treatment on the second, and **order** sandwiches for their room when they arrive.

3 _____

Today, both the business traveller and the leisure guest expect hi-tech guest rooms: flat-screen TVs, docking stations for portable music players, in-room safes with a power point to recharge laptop computers. Rooms also need more power points so guests can plug in their mobile devices.

4 _____

Guests want comfort at an **affordable** rate. They don't want expensive charges for car parking and phone calls, and they don't like **overpriced** breakfasts and in-room fridges. In response, many hotels now leave the fridges empty so guests can bring their own food and drink or order what they want from reception. Other hotels don't put fridges in the guest rooms now. Guests are more satisfied when they check out if the total **charge** is what they expected when they reserved the room.

6 **Complete sentences 1–6 with the words in bold in the article in Exercise 5.**

1 It's a good idea to _____ a room at the top of the hotel. The views are great.

2 The _____ for photocopying is five cents per copy in the business centre.

3 We have to _____ between Paris and London for our next conference.

4 We had a really _____ cappuccino in Piazza San Marco for €14.

5 The hotel has an app that allows guests to _____ room service using their smartphones.

6 Hotels are expensive in Moscow. It's difficult to find _____ accommodation.

7))) **5.5** **Listen to three conversations. What are the people talking about? Write the numbers you hear.**

Speaking

THE RIGHT HOTEL

8 **Work in pairs. Look at the guest profiles. What kind of hotel would you recommend? Decide on a list of the top FIVE facilities you think the hotel needs to offer for each guest profile.**

1

Mr and Mrs Jacobs are a retired couple. She likes to go to a hotel to relax and lose a few kilos. He likes to do outdoor sports, especially golf.

2

Crooks Pharmaceuticals is organizing an event for 100 doctors and their partners. They attend seminars in the morning, have a choice of leisure activities or lectures in the afternoon and socialize in the evening.

> **RESEARCH**
>
> HOTELS IN YOUR AREA
> Choose the nearest big tourist destination. Search online and find a suitable hotel in this town/city for each set of people from Exercise 8. Report back to the class and compare your selections.

PROFESSIONAL SKILLS
DEALING WITH COMPLAINTS

Vocabulary

WHY GUESTS COMPLAIN

1 **Read the statements about guest complaints and tick (✓) the ones you agree with. Compare your ideas with a partner.**

1 ____ Hotel guests complain more now than in the past.

2 ____ It is embarrassing for staff when a guest complains.

3 ____ Negative feedback from guests is useful for a hotel.

4 ____ Staff often feel offended if a guest complains.

5 ____ I would enjoy the opportunity to resolve a guest's complaint.

2 **Complete the text with the adjectives in the box. Use a dictionary to help you.**

> broken   dirty   disappointing   missing   noisy   shabby
> uncomfortable   unhelpful

What hotel guests really hate

Guests are unhappy when hotel facilities don't meet their expectations, e.g. a small swimming pool or a(n) ^{1}_____ view from their bedroom window. They will also be unhappy if the furniture and decor looks old and ^{2}_____, or the electrical equipment in the room is not working – typically the TV remote control. Also, there are complaints if things, e.g. the light switches are ^{3}_____, or if items are ^{4}_____ from the room, e.g. towels or an extra pillow or blanket.

A common complaint is about hygiene standards, e.g. a(n) ^{5}_____ room or bathroom. Guests often complain if they can't get a good night's sleep because of a(n) ^{6}_____ street, or a(n) ^{7}_____ bed. Guests also complain if they feel the staff attitude is rude or ^{8}_____. Finally, there are complaints about unexpected events, e.g. overpriced items on the bill when checking out – even if the bill is correct. In fact, sometimes guests will complain about events completely outside the hotel's control, e.g. weather conditions and flight delays.

3 <u>Underline</u> **the nouns on the right that can be used with the adjective on the left.**

1 noisy	staff, guests, blanket, air conditioning
2 shabby	bill, furniture, room, uniform
3 missing	weather, toiletries, toilet paper, light bulb
4 unhelpful	staff, pool, receptionist, manager

Listening

PUTTING THINGS RIGHT

4 **))) 5.6** **Listen to two conversations. What is each guest unhappy about? Make a list of the problem(s) and solution(s) for each conversation. Does each receptionist deal with the situation well?**

5 Look at the tips in the Professional skills box. Match the useful expressions a–e with the tips 1–5.

a I'm sure the last thing you needed was a hotel room without hot water after your long trip today.

b I see, OK. Yes.

c I'm very sorry that your request was not recorded.

d I'll inform the duty manager about the situation.

e I'll ask the housekeeper to send you up fresh towels immediately.

PROFESSIONAL SKILLS: DEALING WITH COMPLAINTS L.E.A.R.N

1 **L**isten actively. Stay calm and listen without interrupting. Add some 'verbal nods' to show you are listening. ____

2 **E**mpathize. It shows that you understand the situation and the speaker's feelings. ____

3 **A**pologize. An apology is not an admission of fault; it simply says that the intentions were good. ____

4 **R**eact by giving an efficient solution. Try to offer alternatives if it is not possible to give the guest what they want. ____

5 **N**otify a supervisor, if necessary, so he/she can ensure all issues are resolved and the guest is happy. ____

Writing

RESPONDING TO COMPLAINTS

6 The hotel manager responds to the complaint of the second guest in Exercise 4. Complete the email with the words in the box.

apologize   booked   dealt with   feedback   hesitate   refund   sorry   unhelpful

Dear Mr Peterson,

Thank you for your email about your recent experience at our hotel. We welcome
¹_____ from our guests and the opportunity to put things right. I can understand that it was disappointing for you not to receive the room type you requested. Unfortunately, the hotel was fully ²_____ that day and the reception staff put you in a room that needs some renovation.

I am very ³_____ for the inconvenience this caused you. I also ⁴_____ for the ⁵_____ attitude of the staff member who ⁶_____ your complaint at the time. As a gesture of goodwill, I would like to offer you either a full ⁷_____ or a complimentary one-night stay at our hotel.

Please do not ⁸_____ to contact me if you have any further questions or comments.

Best regards,

Sebastian White

Speaking

ROLEPLAY

7 Work in pairs. Student A turn to File 17, page 105. Student B turn to File 25, page 107. Roleplay the situations. Use the tips from the Professional skills box to help you.

8 Write an email replying to one of the complaints in Exercise 7. Use the email in Exercise 6 to help you.

RESEARCH

TYPICAL COMPLAINTS IN HOTELS
What are the most typical complaints in two hotels in your town/city? How do the hotels usually deal with the complaints? Report your findings to the class.

CASE STUDY MAKE A GOOD HOTEL GREAT

CASE STUDY MENU

Aim: To produce an action plan to improve the guest experience at the Apfelsine Hotel.

1 Analyse online guest reviews.
2 Listen to staff opinions.
3 Read staff suggestions.
4 Hold a meeting to create an action plan.

Online guest reviews

1 **Read the online guest reviews for the Apfelsine Hotel in Berlin. How could the hotel improve customer service? How could it improve equipment and facilities? Make a list.**

Apfelsine Hotel

1 We ate in the hotel two nights and the food was fantastic. The only problem was that the service can be a bit slow. They seemed short staffed in the restaurant in the evenings. In general the hotel staff were friendly and helpful but the staff at the café weren't very attentive.

2 We were disappointed that there were no coffee/tea making facilities in the room, no fridge and no air conditioning when we stayed there in the summer. It says in the hotel magazine in the room that this is a 'green hotel' and they try to be environmentally friendly but I'd prefer these facilities next time.

3 The room was spotlessly clean and very comfortable but small – like a lot of European budget hotels. The shower was great. My only small complaint is that the towels were very small and thin! (And I'm not!!)

4 The big issue for me was the service, which was slow and amateurish. I waited for 30 minutes to check in. There was only one receptionist on Friday evening but there were usually two or three people on reception the rest of the weekend. Really disappointing.

5 The only negative thing I can say about the Apfelsine is there is very poor lighting for reading at night but I suppose that is because they use energy saving bulbs.

Staff opinions

2 **))) 5.7** Listen to the staff talking about some problems at the hotel. Complete the manager's notes using ONE or TWO words.

North Americans and Australians usually expect ¹_____. We should offer guests an upgrade to a ²_____ on check-in if one is available. We should also email ³_____ in advance about the small size of standard rooms.

A lot of European guests come for ⁴_____. We should check the ⁵_____ times on Friday evenings and make sure there are enough staff on reception.

Last month some waiting staff were ⁶_____ and we had two new members of the team, who were slower than the others. We should have a list of staff phone numbers to call people who are ⁷_____ in cases of emergency. The ⁸_____ don't speak very good English.

Most guests love the fact that we are a ⁹_____. But some guests are unhappy that they have to come to reception to ask for ¹⁰_____ and shampoo.

Staff suggestions

3 Read the staff suggestions for how to improve the hotel. Make a list of possible improvements.

1
When guests arrive a few hours before the check-in time, let's offer them complimentary coffee and cakes in the restaurant while they're waiting for their room. It's a nice, friendly welcome. And we can take their bags up to the room or store bags if guests want to go out. Also, we get a lot of guests on weekend breaks, so let's have a late checkout option on Sundays.

2
As part of our green hotel plan, we could offer a nice organic breakfast with lots of fresh fruit, juices and nice breads. We could serve breakfast until 1 p.m. – that would make us different from other hotels and guests would love it. Let's put complimentary fruit on the reception desk for guests, too.

3
Why don't we offer our own walking tours of the local neighbourhood? It's a bit different from the typical sights of Berlin. We could also produce our own guide to Berlin for the hotel website with our staff recommendations for tours and restaurants. I think reception staff should ask guests when they arrive if they want any recommendations for things to see and do in the city. It makes us seem more friendly and helpful.

4
We have free Wi-Fi access in the hotel but guests don't always travel with their computers. We could lend them a laptop to use, at no extra charge, if they want to check their email or use the internet while they are in the lobby café. And how about guide books in the lobby and live music in the café at weekends?

TASK

4 **Work in small groups. Look at your list of possible improvements in Exercise 3 and hold a meeting.**

  1 Create a schedule for six main improvements.

  2 Add any suggestions of your own to the list.

  3 Present your action plan to the class.

UNIT 5: KEY WORDS

affordable   apologize
budget   charge   complain
complimentary   disappointing
guest   helpful   laptop   luxury
missing   noisy   refund
request
See DVD-ROM Mini-dictionary

Tourism statistics

1 Complete the questions about international tourism in China. Then match the questions 1–7 with the answers a–g.

1 _____ international visitors did China have in 2010? ___

2 _____ did China earn from international tourism in 2010? ___

3 _____ is the most popular tourist attraction? ___

4 _____ is the Great Wall of China? ___

5 _____ do most visitors to China come from? ___

6 _____ are the world's top tax-free shoppers in Europe? ___

7 _____ does a typical Chinese tourist spend on shopping? ___

a 744 euros

b 56 million

c 8,850 km (5,500 miles)

d 46 billion US dollars

e The Great Wall of China

f Japan

g The Chinese

Checking and confirming

2 Complete the expressions for checking and confirming details.

1 A: ¹_____ do you ²_____ your surname?

B: It's B-R-Y-A-N-T.

2 A: I'm sorry, I didn't catch that. ³_____ you ⁴_____ that number, please?

B: Sure. It's 472 890 112.

3 A: What's your email address?

B: It's Elena dot Newman ⁵_____ gmail ⁶_____ com.

4 A: Could I ⁷_____ those credit card ⁸_____ again?

B: Yes, fine.

Tourism jobs and sectors

3 Put the jobs in the box with the correct tourism sector in the table.

> concierge   driver   entertainer   executive chef   flight attendant
> front office manager   housekeeper   pilot   restaurant manager
> shore excursion manager   tour guide   waiter

Accommodation	Food and Beverage	Transportation	Recreation

4 Complete the adjectives to describe people who ...

1 talk to people in a way that shows they like them   fr __ __ nd __ __

2 are funny and interesting   __ nt __ rt __ __ ni __ g

3 are methodical and plan well   __ rg __ n __ z __ d

4 work quickly and effectively   __ ff __ c __ __ nt

5 like to meet and talk to new people   __ __ tg __ __ ng

6 have a very positive attitude   __ nth __ s __ __ st __ c

Present simple and present continuous

5 Complete the tour manager's story with the present simple or present continuous form of the verbs in brackets.

My main responsibility is designing tailor-made tour packages to meet the needs of different clients. As part of my day-to-day work I ¹_____ (deal with) clients, ²_____ (suggest) travel routes to suit their interests, ³_____ (book) their flights, ⁴_____ (make) hotel reservations and, ⁵_____ (provide) detailed quotations and final itineraries. An important part of the job is also travelling to do research. At present,

I ⁶_____ (explore) new business opportunities in the South American market. It's exciting because I ⁷_____ (not sit) at my computer in the office. Currently I ⁸_____ (visit) new destinations and ⁹_____ (find) great travel routes, places of interest and accommodation to recommend to clients. In addition, I ¹⁰_____ (meet) overseas agents to negotiate new packages.

Tourist information

6 Look at the definitions and write the words connected with tourist information.

Across

1 a thin book that gives information or advertises something

2 a short journey arranged so that a group of people can visit a place

5 when you suggest or recommend what someone should do

6 a piece of paper which gives you information or advertises something

8 the activity of seeing places of interest

9 a popular place to visit or activities to do

Down

1 a holiday for a few days is called a short _____

3 _____ hours – times when a business, e.g. a restaurant or shop is open for people to use it

4 places that are interesting for visitors to see

7 something that has been organized, e.g. a festival or sports competition

Comparatives and superlatives

7 **Complete the tourist information about Venice using the comparative or superlative form of the adjectives in brackets.**

Venice is one of the ¹_____ (interesting) places in the world. However, the summer can be the ²_____ (bad) time to visit. It's sometimes very hot and humid, and there are a lot of tourists. The ³_____ (near) airport is Marco Polo Airport. The Alilaguna water-bus from the airport costs €15 and takes 75 minutes to get to St Mark's Square. Hiring a water-taxi is much ⁴_____ (fast) – 30 minutes – but also ⁵_____ (expensive) – about €100.

Because Venice is on a lagoon, water plays a crucial role in transportation. The vaporetti (water buses) are generally the ⁶_____ (good) way to get around. They are also a lot ⁷_____ (cheap) than private water taxis or gondolas. *Acqua alta* – high water – is a fact of life in Venice. The water level occasionally rises and floods the squares and streets. This usually happens in the ⁸_____ (cold) months, between November and January. You can get an *acqua alta* map at the tourist offices at the railway station or St Mark's. This shows you some ⁹_____ (high) and ¹⁰_____ (dry) routes to take during the flood alerts.

Dealing with enquiries

8 **Match a–h to 1–8 to complete the telephone conversation.**

a Would you like anything else?

b Would you like to book a specific tour?

c Don't worry. We'll show you how to do it when you get here.

d Are you interested in city walks or nature trails?

e You can choose. It's a series of one-hour to full-day trails.

f Right. You'd like some information about the type of tours available.

g We have touch-screen kiosks with printing capabilities here.

h I see. Well, I'd suggest the Waikato river trail. It's suitable for all ages.

A: Hamilton Visitor Centre, Suzanna speaking. How can I help you?

B: Hello, we're interested in walking tours of the Hamilton Region.

A: ¹_____

B: Well, no. I'd like to know some more first.

A: ²_____

B: That's right.

A: ³_____

B: Nature walks but nothing very difficult or energetic.

A: ⁴_____

B: Sounds good. How long is the walk?

A: ⁵_____

B: Great! Where can I get a map of the trail?

A: ⁶_____

B: Oh, I'm not good with computers.

A: ⁷_____

B: OK, thanks. I'll visit the centre this afternoon.

A: ⁸_____

B: No thanks, you've been very helpful.

A: Goodbye and thank you for calling the Visitor Centre.

City tours

9 **Match the tourists' questions 1–6 about The Houses of Parliament in London to the tour guide's answers a–f.**

1 Excuse me, who designed the building?

2 How far is the Tower of London from here?

3 What are 'peers'?

4 Is it OK if I take a few photos here?

5 When did you say it was built?

6 Is there a cafeteria near here?

a I'm afraid not. Visitors can only take photos in Westminster Hall.

b The present building was completed in 1870 but the original palace dates back to 1042.

c The Victorian architect, Sir Charles Barry.

d It's just a few stops on the underground.

e I can recommend the Café Churchill in Parliament Street.

f They are members of the House of Lords.

Past simple

10 Complete this description of the early history of Paris with the correct past simple form of the irregular verbs in brackets.

The site of modern-day Paris was founded by a Celtic tribe called the Parisii. They established a fishing village near the river Seine. Paris's lands ¹_____ (be) prosperous. Later, the area ²_____ (come) under Roman control. They ³_____ (build) a massive fort on the *Ile de la Cité* because the island ⁴_____ (have) the river as additional protection. Under Roman rule the town ⁵_____ (grow) considerably.

The Roman Empire ⁶_____ (fall) in the 5th century. Clovis, king of the Franks, ⁷_____ (make) Paris the capital of his kingdom. The population of the island grew and the city ⁸_____ (become) unsanitary and vulnerable to plague. The rulers moved the city to a new location on the right bank. In 1163, the construction of Notre Dame ⁹_____ (begin). It ¹⁰_____ (take) almost two centuries to complete this masterpiece of gothic architecture.

Package tours

11 Match 1–6 to a–f to make phrases associated with package tours. Then complete the advert for a package tour to India with the correct phrases.

1 airport	**a** tour
2 UNESCO	**b** pack
3 city sightseeing	**c** World Heritage site
4 entry	**d** guide
5 tour	**e** transfers
6 information	**f** tickets

Modal verbs

12 Use a modal verb to make this receptionist's offers and requests sound more polite. Write THREE words.

1 I want to see your passport./_____ your passport, please?

2 Do you want a taxi?/_____ a taxi for you?

3 Spell your surname./_____ your surname, please.

4 Sign here./_____ here, please?

5 What do you want?/_____ help you?

6 Do you want breakfast in the morning?/_____ breakfast in the morning?

Hotel facilities and services

13 Put the hotel facilities and services in the box with the correct group 1–3.

> 24-hour front desk   blanket
> express checkout kiosk   fridge   iron
> laundry service   meeting rooms
> photocopier   printer/fax   safe
> secretarial support   swimming pool

1 Hotel facilities

2 Guest room facilities

3 Business facilities

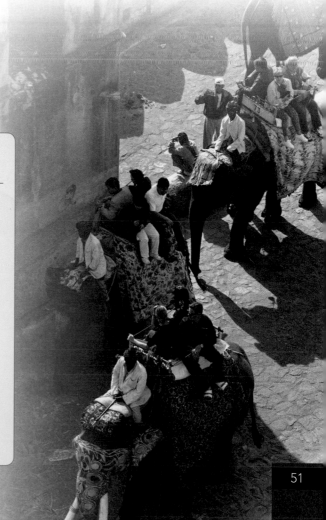

Golden Triangle Tour

Day One: Arrive Delhi. Guests receive welcome gift and free ¹_____ about the tour.
Day Two: Delhi – full day ²_____ of Old Delhi (in the morning) and New Delhi (in the afternoon).
Day Three: Delhi/Agra (210 km)
Shatabdi Express train to Agra with breakfast served on-board.
Agra is the city of Taj Mahal, a ³_____ and the jewel of art in India.
Day Four: Agra/Jaipur (230 km – 5 hr drive)
Optional tour: Wake early morning to visit Taj Mahal at sunrise (at extra cost).
Day Five: Jaipur
Elephant ride to the Amber Fort. In the afternoon visit the Pink City of Jaipur.
Day Six: Jaipur/Delhi (260 km – 5 hr drive)
Price includes: accommodation, breakfast and dinner, ⁴_____ to the Taj Mahal, local ⁵_____ and all activities as per the programme. We provide mineral water throughout the tour. Price does not include: any lunches, airfares and ⁶_____, and travel insurance.

FOOD & BEVERAGE

UNIT MENU

Grammar: countable and uncountable nouns
Vocabulary: food and drink, food orders, catering
Professional skills: meeting customers' needs
Case study: rescue a restaurant

Vocabulary

FOOD AND DRINK

1 **Match 1–6 with a–f. Use a dictionary if necessary. Which word in a–f is not part of the group?**

1	fish	a	mango, lettuce, banana, apple, orange, pineapple
2	meat	b	potato, carrot, onion, cabbage, egg, cucumber
3	fruit	c	milk, cheese, dessert, yoghurt, cream, butter
4	vegetables	d	beef, chicken, prawn, duck, rabbit, lamb
5	dairy products	e	bread, pasta, noodles, rice, breakfast cereal, garlic
6	grain products	f	cod, salmon, tuna, carp, mushroom, trout

2 **Label the photo with the words in the box.**

fork   glass   knife   napkin/serviette   plate   spoon

3 Read the article about Danny Ammaniti's working day. What kind of restaurant does he work in and what is his job?

The Inside Story

I start work at 10 a.m. most days. The waiting staff **set** the tables for lunch and sometimes move tables around if a big party is coming in. Surfers is a large seafood restaurant and we often get group bookings.

Some days, I do training with the new **servers**. I show them how to look after their **station**, how to anticipate guest needs and how to process a customer's **order** and bill.

At 12 p.m. the lunchtime customers start to arrive.

I'm the **front of house** manager for Surfers so I greet people as they arrive. I also walk around making sure they are enjoying their meal, and I'm responsible for dealing with any complaints from unhappy customers.

The evenings are our busiest time with about 195 **covers** a night. Before the evening shift, there is a short meeting with the waiting staff to tell them about the **specials** we want to promote. These promotions can increase sales for the restaurant and their **tips**.

4 Complete the sentences with the words in **bold** from the article in Exercise 3.

1 Waiters are also called _____ in the USA.

2 '_____' refers to how many customers eat during a shift.

3 A server's _____ is the group of tables he or she is responsible for.

4 The dishes that a restaurant is especially promoting are the _____.

5 _____ are extra money that waiters receive from customers for good service.

6 When you _____ a table, you put knives, forks, etc. on it before a meal.

7 The area where the customers are served and waiting staff primarily work is the _____.

8 An _____ is the food and drink requested by a customer.

Listening

IN A SANDWICH BAR

5))) 6.1 Listen to a shop assistant in a sandwich bar and two customers. What do they order? How much do they pay?

6))) Listen again and complete what the shop assistant says. Practise saying the sentences.

1 To eat in or ¹_____?

2 ²_____ sliced bread or a baguette?

3 Would you like any ³_____?

4 And what would you like ⁴_____ with that?

5 ⁵_____ or large?

6 Would you like ⁶_____? We have a great selection of ⁷_____ and muffins.

7 Would you like to pay for that ⁸_____ or ⁹_____?

8 So that's fifteen ¹⁰_____ fifty altogether, please.

7 Work in pairs. What were the customers' replies to the phrases in Exercise 6? Check your answers in audio script 6.1 on page 123.

Speaking

TAKING FOOD ORDERS

8 Work in pairs. Turn to File 18, page 105.

BIG EVENTS

Reading

CATERING FOR A CROWD

1 Work in pairs or small groups. Discuss the questions.

1 When catering for a large group, which is better – a formal dinner or a buffet? Why?

2 Is it better to prepare all the food in advance or to prepare some at the event? Why?

3 How can a catering company avoid long queues for drinks?

2 Read the article and check your answers in Exercise 1.

Sandra Kellerman

Catering for a crowd

When you're planning a large event, which is better – a **sit-down meal** or a buffet? Sandra Kellerman, executive chef and owner of London-based Kellerman Catering, says that buffets are better for parties with thousands of guests. 'Buffets give hungry guests access to food immediately,' she says. She gives the example of the 25th anniversary party of a company, which Kellerman did the catering for the previous week. They set long tables with hors d'oeuvres so that the 3,000 employees could serve themselves when they arrived. Twelve large buffet stations offered both hot and cold items, and chefs at **action stations** provided both food and entertainment – the chefs cooked as guests watched. Kellerman also prepared a lot of food before the event. 'Some items we don't cook until required,' Sandra explains. 'It ensures the culinary team doesn't **run out of** food but that there isn't too much **waste** either.'

The quantity of food necessary is one of the hardest things to judge. The number and type of guests are a guideline. At last week's event 'seventy percent of the guests were men, so we knew the amount of meat was key. Many large events use **disposable** products but at last week's event we used real plates, glassware and **cutlery**,' Kellerman explains. As for the drink service, 'the tables are designed so that there is enough room for the staff to serve three people at a time. Each table had 12 serving staff. All of them had experience working at stadiums and other big venues. These guys know how to make drinks fast.'

3 Read the article in Exercise 2 again and circle the correct answer in italics.

1 Last week's event was a *birthday party / business event / wedding anniversary*.

2 There were *three hundred / thirteen hundred / three thousand* guests.

3 There were twelve tables of *buffet items / hors d'oeuvres / drinks*.

4 Most of the people at the event were *men / women / children*.

5 There were *three staff on each drinks table / twelve drinks tables / twelve staff on each drinks table*.

4 Complete the sentences with the words in **bold** from the article in Exercise 2.

1 A _____ is a food service option offered in which waiters serve food to guests at their tables.

2 _____ are areas at a catered event where guests can watch how their food is cooked.

3 _____ is the knives, forks and spoons used for eating and serving food.

4 When you _____ something, you use all of it and don't have any more.

5 The _____ is the unwanted food after an event.

6 If something is _____, it is intended to be used for a short time and then thrown away.

GRAMMAR: COUNTABLE AND UNCOUNTABLE NOUNS

Countable nouns have a singular and plural form. You can count them, e.g. *apples, eggs, pizzas.*
I have **an** apple.
I have **some** apples.
I have **a lot of** apples.
I don't have **an** apple.
I don't have **many/a lot of** apples.
I don't have **any** apples.
How **many** apples do you have?

Uncountable nouns only have a singular form. You cannot count them, e.g. *water, rice, money.*
I have **some** rice.
I have **a lot of** rice.
I don't have **much/a lot of** rice.
I don't have **any** rice.
How **much** rice do you have?

See Grammar reference, page 114.

5 Study the Grammar box and put the words in the box into the correct group: countable (C), uncountable (U) or both (B). Use a dictionary to help you.

> chocolate   coffee   food   fruit   meal   milk   omelette
> potato   prawn   salt   sandwich   vegetable

6))) **6.2**   Listen and complete Sandra's notes.

> **Client:** P&K Sports
> **Date of event:** ¹_____
> **Expected number of guests:** ²_____
> **Type of event:** ³_____
> **Venue:** Marley's ⁴_____

7)))   Complete the conversation. Then listen again and check your answers.

H = Henry Martins, S = Sandra Kellerman

H: We're expecting ¹____ people and we need ²____ food.

S: Just give me ³____ details. How ⁴____ guests are you expecting?

H: How ⁵____ will it cost?

S: There's ⁶____ space there.

S: So, you don't need ⁷____ beverages?

S: How ⁸____ time do we have to prepare the buffet?

Speaking

CATERING FOR AN EVENT

8 Work in pairs. Student A turn to File 19, page 106. Student B turn to File 39, page 111.

RESEARCH

CATERING FOR EVENTS
Search the internet for a selection of catering menus. Enter the key words: *catering, events, buffet, menu* and find a menu for breakfast, lunch and dinner that you think is interesting, good value and caters for special diets. Present your findings to the class.

6

FOOD & BEVERAGE

A

B

C

D

Speaking

SPECIAL DIETS

1 Work in pairs. Answer the questions about people with special diets.

1 Which of these will a vegetarian eat?
a beef **b** chicken **c** eggs **d** cheese **e** fish **f** nuts

2 Which of these will a vegan eat?
a yoghurt **b** fruit **c** butter **d** vegetables **e** bread **f** pasta

3 Which of these shouldn't you eat if you want to lose weight?
a pizza **b** salad **c** pasta **d** mayonnaise **e** apples

4 Which of these shouldn't a person with a shellfish allergy eat?
a prawns **b** mussels **c** beef **d** clams **e** crab **f** chicken

VOCABULARY: DESCRIBING DISHES

Using adjectives when describing dishes helps to make the descriptions more appealing to customers.

*It is often possible to describe flavours and tastes in English by adding **-y** to the noun, e.g. cheesy, creamy, fishy, fruity, garlicky, meaty, nutty, salty, tasty, etc.*

2 Complete the descriptions with the adjectives in the box. Use a dictionary to help you.

> rich   savoury   spicy   sweet   tender

1 _____ meat is soft. It is easy to cut and eat.
2 _____ food has been flavoured with spices and often has a hot, burning taste.
3 _____ food has a taste similar to sugar.
4 _____ food has a good flavour, and is salty rather than sweet.
5 _____ food usually contains a large amount of cream or butter.

3))) 6.3 Listen and complete the descriptions with the phrases in the box.

> coated in   comes with   made with   marinated in   seasoned with   served with

1 The seafood salad [1]_____ a creamy, lemon dressing [2]_____ olive oil, vinegar, yoghurt, mayonnaise, mustard and fresh lemons.
2 Our Florentine steak is [3]_____ sea salt and black pepper, and [4]_____ white beans.
3 Try our tasty beef Milanese. It's [5]_____ egg and breadcrumbs, and then fried.
4 The chicken is [6]_____ lemon juice, olive oil and garlic for 24 hours, and then barbecued.

4 Look at the photos of different food A–D and match them with the descriptions in Exercise 3.

5 Think of a traditional dish from your country. What are the ingredients? How is it cooked? What is it served with? What adjectives describe the dish? Compare your ideas with a partner.

Listening

SPECIAL REQUESTS

6))) 6.4 What are the three courses of a typical restaurant meal called in the USA? What are they called in the UK? Compare your ideas with a partner. Then listen and check your answers.

7))) 6.5 Listen to a couple ordering a meal in a restaurant. Make notes of the order and special requests.

8))) Listen again. Do you think the waiter did a good job? Why/why not?

PROFESSIONAL SKILLS: MEETING CUSTOMERS' NEEDS

1 Be proactive – try to anticipate the customer's needs. ___

2 Be available – watch each table in your station and be available within a minute or two if a customer needs something. ___

3 Be knowledgeable – some customers ask lots of questions and want suggestions to help them make their choices. Make sure you know the ingredients of the dishes and how they are prepared. ___ / ___

4 Be flexible – some customers have special diets or unique tastes. Show the customer that you can work around their diets and tastes, and respond to requests with a positive attitude. ___

9 Read the advice in the Professional skills box about customer service skills. Match the expressions a–e with the tips 1–4.

   a The lamb comes with baby carrots and roast potatoes.

   b I'll be with you in just a moment.

   c If you like fish, you should try the local sea bass.

   d We could make you a salad without the chicken.

   e Would you like another bottle of water?

Speaking

TODAY'S SPECIALS

10 Work in pairs. Look at Menu One. Student A you are the customer. Think of THREE questions to ask Student B. Student B you are the waiter. Tell Student A about the items on the menu. Invent any details you like.

11 Now swap roles and look at Menu Two.

Menu One

Today's specials

Starters

French onion soup
Seafood special

Mains

Roast lamb
Pan-fried steak with Marsala sauce

Menu Two

Today's specials

Starters

Baked camembert
Garlic mushrooms

Mains

Fresh cod piccata
BBQ chicken

CASE STUDY
RESCUE A RESTAURANT

CASE STUDY MENU

Aim: To rescue a failing restaurant.

1 Read about restaurants in Sydney.

2 Analyse menu items and prices at Katrina's restaurant.

3 Read about dining trends in Australia.

4 Listen to a consultant's advice.

5 Decide what innovations the restaurant needs.

Largest city	Sydney

Population of Sydney over 4 million

Sydney has a cosmopolitan population. The major groups of immigrants are from the UK, China and New Zealand, followed by Vietnam, Lebanon, India, Italy and the Philippines.

The most popular types of restaurants are modern Australian (36%), Chinese (15%), seafood restaurants (9%) and Italian (9%). Ethnic food is very popular as well as a fusion of ethnic and Australian dishes.

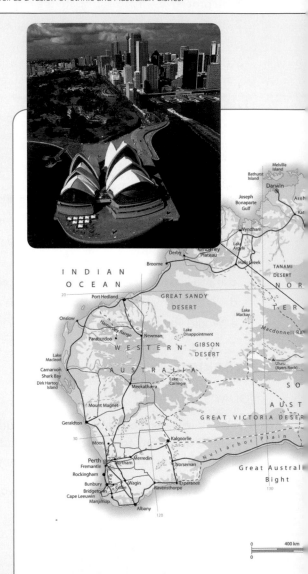

Restaurants in Sydney

1 **Read the information about Sydney. What types of restaurants are popular? Why do you think that is?**

2 **Read the information about Katrina's. What type of restaurant is it? Why do you think it is less popular than in the past?**

Katrina's is a family-owned and family-run restaurant in central Sydney. With 80 covers, the restaurant's main focus is on steak and grilled meat dishes. When the Armstrong family opened the restaurant 20 years ago, it was an instant success. Now Katrina's sales are down 20 percent from last year. The family have to adapt to survive. The restaurant is near several hotels, and is well-located for the tourist trade. Customers are mostly Australian nationals who are on holiday or business in the city, as well as visitors from New Zealand, the UK and the USA.

Sales data

3 **Work in pairs. Student A look at the information below. Exchange information with Student B to complete Katrina's sales data. Student B turn to File 20, page 106.**

e.g. What does the Australian fillet steak cost?

*Menu item	Cost	Menu price	Sold per week
Australian fillet steak	1___	$29	100
T-bone steak	$8.50	$24	2___
Lamb ribs	$10	3___	25
Grilled chicken breast	4___	$23	50
Katrina's beef burger	$5	$21.50	5___
Veggie burger (contains nuts)	$3	6___	15

All main courses are served with chips or baked potatoes. Other vegetables can be ordered as side dishes.

4 **Work in pairs. Look at the sales data in Exercise 3. Which THREE items on the menu should you definitely keep? Which TWO items should you definitely change?**

Dining trends

5 Read the article about dining trends in Australia. What impact could the changes have on Katrina's restaurant?

Diners eating out more

AUSTRALIANS are eating out more than they did last year but new research shows they're also choosing healthier food. The survey found that one in three Australians go out for a meal once a week. The trend is a move away from meat, towards seafood and vegetable dishes. Nearly nine in ten people surveyed think eating healthy is important but 63 percent say it's difficult at restaurants because there aren't enough healthy items. The research also found that people love ethnic food. Chinese, Mediterranean and Latin American cuisines are especially popular.

An expert view

6))) 6.6 Listen to part of a conversation between a consultant and the restaurant owner. Complete the notes from the SWOT analysis.

AUSTRALIA

Strengths

- Excellent quality food
- Great location
- Professional customer service

Weaknesses

- ¹_____ is not popular today
- Too many ²_____ dishes
- Old-fashioned, unattractive ³_____

Opportunities

- Introduce a ⁴_____ at lunchtime
- Reduce ⁵_____ to decrease costs and increase sales of ⁶_____
- Cater to special diets

Threats

- Fluctuating ⁷_____
- Changing attitudes to food and ⁸_____
- A lot of competitors

TASK

7 Work in groups. You are the owners of Katrina's restaurant. Meet to decide the following items.

1 Redesign your menu and add four new main courses and a selection of side orders. Think about healthier options, ethnic dishes and special diets.

2 Design a set menu for a three-course lunch with a choice of three starters, three mains and three desserts.

3 Decide what low-cost changes you can make immediately to the décor and lighting.

4 Decide if you want to give your restaurant a new name and/or concept.

Writing a menu

8 Write the new set lunch menu for Katrina's restaurant. Include the following.

- three starters, three mains and three desserts
- short descriptions of the dishes to make them sound more tasty

UNIT 6: KEY WORDS

bill dessert diet fried grilled homemade made with napkin portion salt serviette set menu shellfish steak tip

See DVD-ROM Mini-dictionary

NATURE TOURISM

UNIT MENU

Grammar: future forms
Vocabulary: tour itineraries, geographical features
Professional skills: structuring a presentation
Case study: be competitive

Listening

A TOUR ITINERARY

1 **What do you know about Costa Rica? Answer the questions and compare your ideas with a partner.**

    1 What does 'Costa Rica' mean and where is it?

    2 Why is it a popular tourist destination?

2 **))) 7.1** **A tour director is talking to a group about their itinerary in Costa Rica. Listen to Part One and correct the tour director's notes. There are FIVE corrections.**

Day One: San José Arrive at hotel. Welcome reception and lunch. **Day two: Quepos** **Accommodation:** small hotel Spend the day at Parque Nacional Manuel Antonio on the Pacific coast. **Things to do:** wildlife spotting, swimming and sunbathing **Remember:** wear a bathing suit – we'll provide towels **Important note:** Don't feed the monkeys.	**Day three: Quepos** **Options:** 1 trek with a nature guide to Tocori Waterfall 2 kayak along the coastline, scuba diving **Day four: Quepos** Tour of Rainmaker Conservation Project **Options:** 1 walk in the forest to a lake – can swim there 2 nature trail with suspension bridges between the treetops – wildlife spotting, learn about the rainforest from a local guide

GRAMMAR: FUTURE FORMS

Use the present continuous and **going to** + infinitive for future plans and arrangements.
We're going to spend tomorrow at Parque Nacional Manuel Antonio.
Note: We generally use the present continuous if times and dates are mentioned.
We're leaving San José at 6 a.m. tomorrow.

Use **will** for predictions about facts and events expected to be true in the future.
I'm sure you'll see a lot of crocodiles.
If you're interested in wildlife, you'll love the jungle tour.

See Grammar reference, page 115.

3 **Study the Grammar box. Look at audio script 7.1 on page 124 and underline FOUR more examples of future forms.**

4))) 7.2 **Listen to Part Two and complete the itinerary.**

> **Day five: Jacó**
> **Pacific Rainforest aerial tram**
> - ride through the ¹_____ on open-air gondolas
> - fabulous views of the ²_____
>
> **Day six: Tárcoles**
> **Highway 34**
> - ³_____ from Tárcoles village up the river to see the crocodiles
> **Warning:** these reptiles can get ⁴_____
>
> **Day seven: Jacó**
> **Parque Nacional Carara**
> - some of the most varied forests and ⁵_____ in Costa Rica
>
> **Day eight: Jacó**
> **Morning:** free to explore, take a ⁶_____ lesson, go shopping for souvenirs or relax
> **Afternoon:** fly back to San José from Jacó airport
> **Days nine and ten:** San José

5 Read the new messages 1–3 for the tour director and complete the announcement with the verbs in the box in the correct future form.

> **1** Flight to Quepos delayed by three hours tomorrow morning. Trip to Manuel Antonio National Park is now only for half a day.

> **2** Great idea! Yes, offer the tour group a farewell cocktail on the last night in San José.

> **3** I'm very sorry but there are no rooms available at our nature lodge on the first night of your stay. The good news is we have found you alternative accommodation at Hotel Vista Mar for one night at no extra charge. Your group can transfer to Selva Lodge for the other two nights.

> enjoy   have   join   leave   meet   spend   stay   transfer

Here are some changes to our itinerary. First of all, our flight tomorrow morning is ¹_____ three hours later. So, we are ²_____ in the hotel lobby at 9 a.m. not 6 a.m. and we're ³_____ half a day at Manuel Antonio National Park. I'm sure you'll ⁴_____ the park very much.

There's a change to the accommodation on day five. We are ⁵_____ at Hotel Vista Mar for the first night. Then, we are ⁶_____ to La Selva Nature Lodge for the next two nights. And finally, we're ⁷_____ farewell drinks here on the last night. I hope you'll ⁸_____ us then.

Speaking

PLANNING AN ITINERARY

6 Work in pairs. Plan a short itinerary in your country that starts tomorrow. Include the following details.

- starting point, route and locations
- tour length (e.g. three nights/four days, six nights/seven days, nine nights/ten days)
- activities (e.g. gentle activities, adventurous activities)
- type(s) of accommodation (e.g. campsite, nature lodge, luxury hotel)

7 Present your itinerary to another group or to the class.

> **RESEARCH**
>
> POPULAR OUTDOOR ACTIVITIES
> Find out which outdoor activities are popular in your country or region. Present some facts and figures to your class about favourite locations, equipment used and typical cost of these activities.

KENYA

Reading

WHY VISIT KENYA?

1 Read the text about Kenya and find the places in the box on the map.

> Lake Victoria   Mombasa   Mount Kenya   Nairobi
> The Great Rift Valley   The Indian Ocean

Why visit Kenya?

Kenya has a spectacular natural diversity, from tropical forests and deserts to mountains and **savannahs**. There are many activities on offer to suit your tastes, preferences and budget.

The country is divided from north to south by the Great Rift Valley, which is wide and shallow in the north, and deeper and surrounded by cliffs further south. The north is a region of deserts where travellers can go on camel safaris. West of the valley, savannah **plains** descend to the sandy **shores** of Lake Victoria.

The plains of the southern savannahs are the most popular regions for safari trips. Kenya's national parks and **game reserves** are a paradise for wildlife enthusiasts who want to see the Big Five: leopard, lion, elephant, rhino and buffalo.

The capital, Nairobi, is located in the south on a 1,500 m high plateau. Mount Kenya (Kirinyaga), 150 km north to northeast of the capital, is Africa's second highest mountain.

Mombasa, Kenya's second largest city, is in the southeast next to the Indian Ocean. The tropical **coastline** with its palm-lined beaches is a popular attraction for visitors who want to sunbathe and explore the underwater life of the **coral reefs** along the clear blue Indian Ocean.

2 Complete the definitions 1–6 with the words in bold from the text in Exercise 1.

1 _____: large flat areas of land covered with grass; found in hot countries

2 _____: large areas of land designed for wild animals to live in safely

3 _____: large areas of flat land

4 _____: line of rocks or sand just above or just below the surface of the sea

5 _____: land along the edge of a sea, lake or wide river

6 _____: shape of the land on the coast, especially as seen from the air

Speaking

DESCRIBING GEOGRAPHICAL FEATURES

3 **))) 7.3** **Listen and complete the dimensions of two natural wonders of Africa.**

1 Victoria Falls: Height _____ Width _____

2 Fish River Canyon: Length _____ Width _____ Depth _____

4 **Look at audio script 7.3 on page 124 and find the adjectives for the dimensions in Exercise 3.**

5 **Work in pairs. Student A look at the information in the fact file below. Student B turn to File 21, page 106. Ask and answer questions to complete the missing information.**

KENYA

Fact file: The natural wonders of Africa

The **Sahara Desert** is the largest hot desert in the world. It covers [1]_____ countries and there are sand dunes as high as [2]_____ m.

The **Red Sea Reef** off the coasts of Egypt, Sudan, and Eritrea is [3]_____ km long. There are more than [4]_____ species of fish here.

Mount Kilimanjaro in northern Tanzania is the highest mountain in Africa at [5]_____ m. The second highest mountain, Mount Kenya, has three peaks over 4,900 m.

The **Serengeti** plains are located in north Tanzania and southwest Kenya. Some 70 larger mammal species, including wildebeest, zebras and buffalo, and about 500 bird species are found here.

Aldabra Atoll, a coral island in the shape of a ring in the Indian Ocean, is 34 km long and 14.5 km wide.

6 **Work in small groups. Complete 1–4.**

1 Select five natural wonders in your country or continent and research them.

2 Write a short description of each wonder, including where it is in the country or continent and its dimensions.

3 Present your selection to the class.

4 Vote on the best selection in the class.

PROFESSIONAL SKILLS
STRUCTURING A PRESENTATION

Reading

PRESENTING MASURIA

1 Where in your country can visitors enjoy nature tourism and water sports?

2 Read the text about the Masuria region in Poland and circle the correct options in italics.

Masuria

The northeastern region of Poland is famous for its many lakes. The landscape was formed by [1]*glaciers / rivers* in the last ice age about 15,000 years ago. It is mostly hilly, with connecting [2]*mountains / lakes* and rivers. Forests cover about 30 percent of the [3]*border / area* and Lake Śniardwy is 106 square km and the biggest lake in Poland. UNESCO has listed Lake Łuknajno as a World Biosphere Reserve. The region's economy depends mostly on [4]*natural / nature* tourism and agriculture. Olsztyn and Białystok are the major cities in northeastern Poland but Mikołajki is the summer capital, with a large [5]*marina / pool* where you can hire yachts, canoes and motorboats. The region is popular with holidaymakers and [6]*sailing / water* sports enthusiasts.

Listening

PRESENTING A NATURE RESORT

3))) 7.4 Janusz Karpowicz is at a tourism fair. He is presenting the Masuria Paradise resort to some tour operators. Listen to Part One and complete the notes.

Masuria Paradise

Region: [1]_____
Type of accommodation: [2]_____
The lodges are built by a small lake and have spectacular [3]_____ across the water.
Water sports: canoeing, [4]_____ and [5]_____
The lake has a swimming area that is [6]_____ for [7]_____.
Outdoor activities: [8]_____, [9]_____, tours of the local nature reserves or mushroom-picking in the forest.
There is also a programme of evening [10]_____.

4)))) **7.5** Listen to Part Two and complete the notes.

> Location of Masuria Paradise: ¹_____   Advantages of the resort: ³_____
> Mobile phone coverage: ²_____   Approved by: ⁴_____

5 Would you recommend the Masuria Paradise nature resort to groups 1–4? Why/why not? Compare your ideas with a partner.

  1 a large school group of 16–17-year-olds

  2 a coach tour of senior citizens

  3 a group of managers on a team-building weekend

  4 a group of two families with young children

6 Put the words in the correct order. Look at audio script 7.4 on page 124 and check your answers.

  a northeast / I'm / Tourism / from the / Association. / Janusz Karpowicz / Poland

  b it's the / in / Europe. / think / lake-land area / most beautiful / We

  c to take / now. / happy / Right, / questions / I'll be / any

  d unique? / One of / is … / the Masuria Paradise resort / the reasons / So why is

  e Masuria Paradise / stunningly / Poland. / northeast / It's the / beautiful / in

  f the land of / Have / a thousand lakes? / ever / heard of / you

7 Read the tips in the Professional skills box and match phrases a–f in Exercise 6 with the tips 1–6.

> ### PROFESSIONAL SKILLS: STRUCTURING A PRESENTATION
>
> **1** Before you start, introduce yourself and say what you are going to talk about. ___
> **2** Start your presentation with a question or an interesting fact or figure. ___
> **3** Explain why your product or services is/are different from the competition. ___
> **4** Use superlative forms, e.g. *the best*. ___
> **5** Use interesting adjectives and adverbs to sound enthusiastic, e.g. *great, amazing, spectacular.* ___
> **6** Give people an opportunity to ask questions at the end. ___

Speaking

PRESENTING OUTDOOR ACTIVITIES

8 Work in pairs. Try to 'sell' your favourite city or region to your partner using the expressions in 1–6.

  1 'People say that ___.'

  2 '___ is a great place for people who enjoy ___.'

  3 'The best place to eat is ___. The food is ___!'

  4 'If you love ___ing, you'll love my town.'

  5 'You must visit ___ because it's amazing!'

  6 'So, if you love ___ and want to see ___, then come to ___.'

9 Work in pairs. Prepare a presentation on a city or region you know well. Take turns to present to the class. Prepare questions to ask about the other presentations. Then vote on the best presentation.

  • Give information about outdoor activities in or near your home town.

  • Use expressions for presentations.

  • Be prepared to answer any questions at the end.

CASE STUDY BE COMPETITIVE

Aim: To make Weru Nature Tours more competitive.

1 Compare Weru Nature Tours with a competitor.

2 Listen to some customer feedback and suggestions.

3 Decide what changes to make to Wero Nature Tours.

4 Offer a customized tour and give a short presentation.

Population	4.3 million
Capital	Wellington
Adventure sports capital	Queenstown
Area	270,530 square km (104,420 square miles) – two large islands and many smaller ones
Climate	the north is sub-tropical and the south is sub-Antarctic

Wero Nature Tours v. Manu Adventures

1 **Work in pairs. Read advertisements A and B for the two tour companies and answer the questions.**

1 What kind of activities do Wero Nature Tours offer?

2 What kind of packages do Manu Adventures specialize in?

3 Which activities sound more exciting to you?

A

Wero Nature Tours

Wero Nature Tours have been an established company based in Queenstown for 15 years. Queenstown is New Zealand's top adventure tourism destination because of the many sports on offer. 'Wero' means 'challenge' in Maori. Wero Nature Tours offer outdoor activities like mountain biking, *tramping and white-water rafting. We specialize in team-building experiences for individuals, families and companies, and we have many repeat customers.

*tramping = New Zealand word for trekking

WERO
Nature Tours

NEW ZEALAND

DK

B

Manu Adventures

'Manu' is Maori for 'bird'. Based in Queenstown, this young, dynamic company offers tour packages with aerial sports including bungee jumping, tandem skydiving, as well as more relaxing outdoor activities, e.g. hot air ballooning, *flightseeing. Manu specialize in extreme sports and offer exciting adventure packages as well as customized itineraries. We also have an excellent safety record.

*flightseeing = sightseeing by air

2 Work in pairs. Compare the information about the two companies. Answer the questions.

1 Which company do you think offers the best value for money?

2 Which activities are suitable for a) families with young children b) corporate groups c) individuals interested in high-adrenalin experiences?

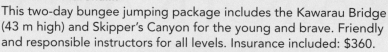

Wero Nature Tours Price list

Nevis white-water rafting: $190
Kawarau River Tour, white-water rafting and tramping: $298
Mountain biking: Coronet Peak $25–$50; Lake Wakatipu $50–75
Tramping: various routes in Aspiring National Park $25–$50

(prices per person, per day, in NZ$)

Manu Adventures

*Group discounts are available for all tours

Total Kiwi Adrenalin
This two-day bungee jumping package includes the Kawarau Bridge (43 m high) and Skipper's Canyon for the young and brave. Friendly and responsible instructors for all levels. Insurance included: $360.

Snow Bird & Phoenix Tour
This one-day adventurous flightseeing tour includes amazing aerial views from Lake Wakatipu, plus a breathtaking hot air balloon safari. If it's your first time in New Zealand, this is the tour for you: $545.

The Extreme Manu Experience
This fantastic two-day package includes something for everyone, with bungee jumping, tandem skydiving, as well as our hot air balloon safari and spectacular flightseeing tour of the Remarkable Mountains. Ideal for groups. You'll never forget it! $995 (insurance included).

(prices per person, per day, in NZ$)

Customer Feedback

3))) 7.6 Wero have lost 20% of their sales since Manu Adventures opened last year. Listen to some customer feedback and complete the table.

Wero Nature Tours Customer Feedback

	Instructors	Equipment	Suggestions for new activities
1	*friendly, helpful*		
2			
3			

TASK

4 Work in pairs. You are going to improve Wero Nature's offer. Look at the tour in the Writing bank on page 101 to help you.

1 Choose activities from the list below and add some of your own.

2 Create three new packages. Decide what will be attractive and different about them.

3 Name and price the packages. If you need to invest in new equipment, staff, etc. you will need to charge more.

4 Write descriptions for the company website. Include information about prices, discounts, etc.

- *bungee jumping
- dolphin watching
- Fiordland National Park
- *flightseeing in Fiordland
- jet boating on Shotover river

- glacier trekking
- *tandem skydiving
- *SNUBA® diving
- *skurfing on a river

*Additional insurance and new trainers are required for these activities.

5 Present your packages to the class.

UNIT 7: KEY WORDS

canoeing   cliff   coast   desert
forest   landscape   nature reserve
reef   scuba diving   sunbathing
trekking   valley   waterfall
white-water rafting   wildlife

See DVD-ROM Mini-dictionary

8

AIR TRAVEL

UNIT MENU

Grammar: modal verbs
Vocabulary: airport facilities, giving directions
Professional skills: dealing with difficult passengers
Game: The Airport Game

Vocabulary

BIG NUMBERS/AIRPORT FACILITIES

1))) **8.1** **Listen to the information about Heathrow Airport in London and complete the facts and figures. What makes Heathrow Airport unusual?**

Heathrow is one of the world's busiest airports. There are over [1]___ flights a day, carrying on average [2]___ passengers. Heathrow deals with nearly [3]___ arriving and departing passengers every year. And most incredible of all, Heathrow has only [4]___ runways for almost [5]___ flights a year, making it the busiest international air space in the world.

2 **Work in pairs. Find out more about Heathrow Airport. Student A turn to File 22, page 106. Student B turn to File 27, page 108. Take turns to ask and answer questions to complete the information.**

3 **Match the facilities with the airport signs. Can you think of any more airport facilities?**

1	2	3	4	5	6	7	8

> Baggage reclaim   Check-in desks   Currency Exchange   Customs   Gates
> Luggage trolleys   Passport control   Toilets

4 **Match the American English words 1–8 with the British English words in the box.**

> car hire   car park   cash machine   check-in desk
> hand baggage   lift   toilet   trolley

1 ATM
2 car rental
3 carry-on bags
4 cart

5 check-in counter
6 elevator
7 parking lot
8 restroom

Listening

WHERE ARE THEY?

5 Complete 1–5 with the words and phrases in the box. Where in an airport would you hear these words/phrases and who would be speaking them?

> baggage   boarding pass   fare   remove   sharp   tray

1 The ¹_____ is 31 euros to the airport.

2 Can I see your passport and ²_____, please?

3 Do you have any ³_____ to check in?

4 Can you ⁴_____ your jacket, please, and put it in a ⁵_____?

5 Are you carrying any liquids or ⁶_____ objects?

6)))) 8.2   Listen to three conversations. Where does each conversation take place and what are the problems?

Speaking

GIVING DIRECTIONS

7)))) 8.3   Listen to four passengers at the airport information desk and complete the expressions.

1 Go right here. Then go ¹_____ past the check-in desks. When you get to the end, ²_____. They are ³_____ just after the lifts.

2 If you want Tourist Information, you should ⁴_____ the terminal, ⁵_____ the café and the airline offices, and then turn right. It's on the left ⁶_____ the car rental offices and the hotel reservation desk.

3 Then take the escalators or the lift to the first floor to ⁷_____ security. Then ⁸_____ for your gate number.

4 Go through the exit door ⁹_____ and turn right. You'll see the bus stop just ¹⁰_____ the terminal building.

8 Work in pairs. You work at the airport information desk. Look at the map and take turns to ask for and give directions.

1 Student A ask for directions to the taxis, the meeting point, Terminal 2 and the shops.

2 Student B ask for directions to the security checkpoint, the cash machines, the car rental offices and a place where you can get something to eat and drink.

First floor: Departures

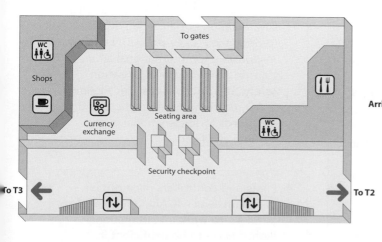

Ground floor: Arrivals and check-in

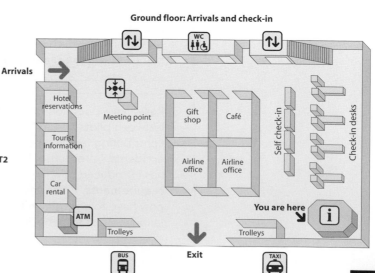

FLIGHT SAFETY

Listening

AIR TRAFFIC CONTROL

1 What do you know about the job of an air traffic controller? What do they do during the different stages of a flight 1–3? Compare your ideas with a partner.

1 take-off   **2** during the flight   **3** landing

2)))8.4   Listen to an interview with an air traffic controller and check your answers in Exercise 1.

Reading

THE ICAO

3 Read the journalist's notes from a press conference given by the ICAO (International Civil Aviation Organization). What was the conference about?

a a new organization responsible for aviation safety

b a language test for pilots and air traffic control

c new licences for international airports

1 Every few seconds a plane takes off or lands somewhere in the world. The pilots who fly the planes and the air traffic control (ATC) services which direct the planes all use the same systems.

2 Systems established by International Civil Aviation Organization, ICAO, (pronounced 'I-kay-oh') – UN agency responsible for international air transport and improving aviation safety. 188 member countries follow ICAO recommended practices and **standards** for international pilot training and licensing.

3 Research – poor communication between pilots and ATCs is a contributing factor in some fatal accidents. In response, ICAO has introduced new language **requirements**. Pilots and ATCs now have to pass a new English language test to get a licence.

4 Pilots and controllers must obtain minimum level – ICAO Operational Level 4 – to work on international flights. Have to be **proficient** in ICAO **phraseology** (aviation English) and **plain English**. Have to take test every three years to keep licence.

4 Complete the sentences with the words in bold from the texts in Exercise 3.

1 The _____ are the levels of quality that the ICAO expects of its members.

2 A phrase used to describe language which is clear, simple and direct is _____.

3 The ways words are used in a particular speciality or subject is its _____.

4 Essential things that you need because of a rule or law are _____.

5 If you are _____ in something, you are skilled and experienced.

GRAMMAR: MODAL VERBS

1 Obligation
Use **must** and **have to** when something is a legal obligation or absolutely necessary.
*Pilots **must** renew their qualification every three years.*
*Air traffic controllers **have to** speak English if requested.*

2 Prohibition
Use **be (not) allowed to** and **mustn't** when something is not permitted.
*The English test **mustn't** be aviation phraseology only.*
*Student pilots are **not allowed to** carry passengers.*

Note: Use **don't have to** when something is not necessary.

3 Permission
Use **be allowed to** when something is permitted.
*Are pilots **allowed to** do the test online?*
Note: Use **can** also for permission.

4 Advice
Use **should** to give recommendations and advice.
*Member countries of the ICAO **should** follow its standards but there is no legal obligation.*

See Grammar reference, pages 115 and 116.

5 Study the Grammar box. Complete the sentences about passenger regulations with the modal verb forms in the box.

| allowed to   must   mustn't   should |

1 Passengers _____ read the aircraft safety card.

2 Passengers _____ fasten their seatbelts during take-off and landing.

3 You aren't _____ smoke on board the plane.

4 You _____ block the emergency exits.

5 Passengers are not _____ use their mobile phones during the flight.

6 You _____ inflate your life jacket inside the aircraft.

Speaking

RULES AND REGULATIONS

6 Work in pairs. Write rules and regulations for TWO of the situations 1–4. Include ONE piece of advice with *should*.

1 passengers on a plane or coach

2 visitors to a museum

3 trekkers in the jungle or mountains

4 tourists in the desert

7 Read your rules and regulations to the rest of the class. Can they guess the situation?

RESEARCH

ATCs IN YOUR COUNTRY
Find out more about air traffic controllers in your country. Use these ideas to help you: entry qualifications, length and cost of training, salary range, working hours and types of jobs.

PROFESSIONAL SKILLS
DEALING WITH DIFFICULT PASSENGERS

Listening

TYPICAL SITUATIONS

1 What personal qualities do you need to work for an airline? In what situations do passengers get angry or upset? Compare your ideas with a partner.

2)))·8.5 Listen to three conversations between airline staff and passengers and answer the questions.

1 Where does the conversation take place: on the ground or in the air?

2 What is the problem in each conversation?

3 How would you describe the passenger(s), e.g. angry, demanding, nervous, noisy, rude?

4 Which situation is most difficult to deal with and why?

3))) Listen again and complete 1–8. Look at audio script 8.5 on pages 125–126 and check your answers.

1 Listen, _____ keep the noise down a bit?

2 I'm _____ the 'fasten seat belt' sign is on now. You see, we're descending into Madrid soon.

3 It _____ long before we land.

4 We're just passing through an area of turbulence. _____, it's perfectly normal.

5 Please _____ everything is fine.

6 _____, sir. I'm afraid that suitcase is too big to take on board.

7 I'm _____ we'll have to check your bag in here at the boarding gate.

8 Yes, there is a _____.

4))) Listen again. Do you think the staff deal with the difficult situations well? Why/Why not? Compare your ideas with a partner.

PROFESSIONAL SKILLS: DEALING WITH DIFFICULT PASSENGERS

Empathize
Show understanding of the issue(s) and identify with the passenger's feelings.
I can see you are unhappy about this.

Apologize
When you apologize to a passenger, they feel better about the situation.
I apologize for the delay.

Explain the situation
Give reasons. Passengers are more cooperative when they are informed.
I'm afraid the duty-free sales are closed now. You see, we're descending into Milan soon.

Find a solution
Ask what the problem is. Offer a solution or have the passenger suggest a solution.
I'll put your bag in another compartment.

5 Work in pairs. Study the Professional skills box and take turns saying the expressions. Look at audio script 8.5 on pages 125–126 for similar expressions.

Speaking

ROLEPLAY

6 Work in pairs. Student A look at the information below. Student B turn to File 23, page 107. Roleplay the situations.

Student A

1 You work at the check-in desk at the airport. The check-in baggage allowance is one bag and 20 kilos per passenger. Excess baggage costs ten euros per kilo. This passenger's suitcase weighs 30 kilos.

2 You are a passenger. You are flying from New York to London and you are not satisfied. Your flight is taking off two hours late, the plane is full and you are in the middle seat between a big, sweaty man and a woman with a crying baby. You ordered a special vegetarian meal.

7 Which situation in Exercise 6 was the most difficult to deal with and why? Compare your ideas with a partner.

Writing

RESPONDING TO COMPLAINTS

8 Complete the email response with the words in the box. Not all of the words are used.

> apologize   apology   behalf   confidence   for   inconvenience
> opinion   regret   sorry   understand

From:	giselle.bauer@LNYair.com
To:	cheng.koon-sung@microsun.com
Subject:	Complaint about service
Date:	December 10

Dear Mr Cheng,

On ¹_____ of our airline, I apologize ²_____ the problems on your recent flight with us from New York to London. I can ³_____ how frustrating it is when your flight is delayed. Unfortunately, bad weather conditions created delays and cancellations across the country that day.

I am also very ⁴_____ you did not receive the special meal that you requested. Thank you for bringing this matter to our attention. We want to make travel with us a convenient and trouble-free experience for our passengers but we failed on this occasion.

As a gesture of apology for the ⁵_____, I am adding 1,000 bonus miles to your frequent flyer account. I hope that you will fly with us again soon so that we can have an opportunity to restore your ⁶_____ in us.

Sincerely,

Giselle Bauer

Customer Relations

THE AIRPORT GAME

START

1

A passenger arrives in the wrong terminal. Explain the situation. Give directions and the estimated time to get to the correct terminal building.

2 →

A passenger arrives at your check-in desk with an out-of-date passport. What do you say?

3 →

A passenger needs to check in baggage. The charge is 30 euros. The passenger didn't know about this and complains. Be polite and diplomatic.

4 →

The flight is overbooked. Inform the passenger. Offer some compensation if the person will agree to take a later flight.

FINISH

24

Congratulations! It's the end of another busy day at the airport. See you tomorrow!

23

At the information desk, a passenger asks how to get into town. Explain the transport options, times and prices.

←

21

Go back three spaces.

→

22 ↑

At the baggage reclaim, a passenger can't find her baggage. Take the details. Go back one space.

20 ↑

After a 30-minute wait for stairs to the plane, the passengers inside are angry. One person tries to open the emergency exit. What do you do?

19

After landing, there is a long delay bringing the stairs and transfer buses to the plane. Make an announcement to the tired passengers.

←

18

A passenger asks, 'Can I use my laptop on-board?' What are the safety regulations?

←

17

The flight is being diverted to another airport because of a summer storm. Make the announcement to passengers. Go back one space.

←

Work in pairs. You work at Elmbridge International Airport. Follow the instructions and play the game.

Instructions

1 Toss a coin to move. Heads = move one square. Tails = move two squares.
2 Follow the instructions on each square. Deal with each situation efficiently and politely. Use appropriate professional expressions.
3 If you land on a square your partner landed on before, move onto the next new square.
4 The first person to complete all the tasks in a professional way is the winner.

5
You are crossing the terminal. An elderly passenger stops you and asks where the nearest lift is. Give directions and offer assistance.

6
An angry passenger arrives on the wrong day and misses the flight. Deal with him/her calmly and politely.

7 →
At the security checkpoint, inform passengers which things they can and can't take in their hand baggage.

8
Complete what the security personnel say: 'Please ___ your jacket, your ___ and ___. And put them in the ___ for X-ray.'
↓

10
Inform the passengers about a flight delay. Apologize and give a reason for the delay, e.g. weather conditions. Go back one space.
↓

9
Go back three spaces.
←

11 →
Describe the restaurant and other airport facilities for a group of passengers whose flight is delayed. Answer any questions.

12
You are a flight attendant. During the pre-flight safety announcement, some passengers are laughing and talking. What do you say to them?
↓

16
A passenger complains that a child in the seat behind is kicking the back of his seat. What do you do?
←

15
Go back three spaces.
←

14
During the flight there is a lot of turbulence. A passenger tells you he is very frightened. What do you say to calm him down?
←

13
The plane is waiting to take off. A passenger tells you that her young child needs to go to the toilet. What do you do?
←

UNIT 8: KEY WORDS

air traffic controller baggage
delay demanding departures
diplomatic fare
flight attendant gate land
pilot polite remove
security checkpoint take-off
See DVD-ROM Mini-dictionary

9 HOTEL OPERATIONS

UNIT MENU

Grammar: present perfect
Vocabulary: housekeeping supplies, refurbishment, checking a hotel bill
Professional skills: checking out
Case study: choose a contractor

Reading

HOUSEKEEPING

1 Tick (✓) the jobs below that you think an executive housekeeper (EHK) does.

1 ___ clean rooms   **4** ___ plan window cleaning and building work

2 ___ inspect rooms   **5** ___ supervise housekeepers

3 ___ wash laundry   **6** ___ iron uniforms

2 Read the extracts from an interview with Cindy Seng, an EHK for a luxury hotel in Malaysia. Check your answers in Exercise 1.

Interview with an EHK

1 _____

I was working as Assistant Housekeeping Manager at the Hyatt Kuantan in Malaysia and after 18 months I was promoted to EHK. I had to learn about hiring and supervising housekeepers, as well as maintenance and laundry staff. There was a very old laundry plant with machinery that broke down daily, which gave me a few headaches.

2 _____

Our priority is the guest rooms: the hotel has 340 rooms, 64 suites and two presidential suites, and I have to inspect them all! Cleaning the crystal chandeliers in the lobby area is difficult, so we do that during low occupancy periods or at night so we don't disturb the guests. Window cleaning and building work are always huge jobs, so we plan these every three months.

3 _____

We've had guests who try to cook in their rooms on camping stoves and some bring pets into the hotel, which they can't do. But the worst thing is when a guest checks out and the room looks as if it has been turned upside down – that can take hours to clean.

4 _____

Guests have taken bath towels and anti-theft clothes hangers, duvets and even hairdryers on walls!

5 _____

Housekeeping today is not just about cleaning. Everything is controlled electronically. You need to understand numbers, purchasing and budgets, and know how staff productivity and your department's expenses affect the hotel's costs and profits. But there are a lot of hotel companies who only see HK as the cleaning department!

3 Read the extracts in Exercise 2 again and match questions a–e with the correct paragraph 1–5.

a What are the biggest cleaning jobs?

b What was your first job as an EHK?

c How has housekeeping management changed in recent years?

d Have guests ever stolen unusual things from the rooms?

e Have you ever had any messy guests?

Vocabulary

HOUSEKEEPING SUPPLIES

4 **Match words 1–6 with categories a–f. Use a dictionary to check the pronunciation.**

1 sheet, pillow case, duvet, blanket, mattress
2 hairdryer, toiletries, towels, mirror, soap
3 rug, lamp, armchair, bedside table, clothes hanger
4 wash, clean, vacuum, dust, mop
5 broom, mop, dustpan and brush, vacuum cleaner
6 detergent, stain remover, disinfectant, polish, bleach

a cleaning products
b bed linen
c cleaning equipment
d bathroom items
e guest room items
f cleaning verbs

GRAMMAR: PRESENT PERFECT

Make the **present perfect** using *have/has* + past participle of the verb. Many past participles are **regular**, e.g. *studied, worked, started* but some are **irregular**, e.g. *had, done, taken*.

Use the present perfect to talk about life experiences, often with words like *ever* and *never*.
*Have you **ever** had any messy guests?*
*He has **never** worked in housekeeping before.*

Use the present perfect to talk about recent changes or events, usually with words like *just, already, yet, recently, this week/month*. *Just* and *already* go before the past participle but *yet* goes at the end. Use *yet* only in negatives and questions.
*We've renovated the hotel **this year**.*
*Have you cleaned the lobby **yet**?*
*They've **just** opened some new apartments.*

See Grammar reference, page 116.

5 **Study the Grammar box. Which questions in Exercise 3 are in the present perfect?**

6 **Put the verbs in brackets in the correct present perfect form. Use contractions where possible.**

1 One out of five Americans ¹_____ (take) a hotel towel, clothes hanger or ashtray.
2 She ²_____ already ³_____ (train) as a Housekeeping Manager.
3 ⁴_____ he ⁵_____ (iron) his uniform?
4 We ⁶_____ (never/clean) the chandeliers before.
5 He ⁷_____ (not/do) the fifth floor yet.
6 ⁸_____ you ⁹_____ (make) the beds yet?

Listening

HOUSEKEEPING INSPECTION

7 **))) 9.1** **EHK Ray is checking the work of Matilda, a new housekeeper. Think of THREE questions he could ask her. Listen and check your answers.**

8 **)))** **Listen again and complete the sentences.**

1 Matilda is cleaning rooms on the ___ floor.
2 She still has ___ rooms to clean.
3 Ray asks Matilda to clean the ___ again and go over the corners.
4 He asks if she has counted the towels, linen and ___.
5 The last guests have left a tip of ___ dollars.

Speaking

THE NEW HOUSEKEEPER

9 **Work in pairs. An EHK is checking a new housekeeper's work before the guests arrive. Student A turn to File 24, page 107. Student B turn to File 36, page 110.**

REFURBISHMENT

Listening

TRENDS IN HOTEL REFURBISHMENT

1))) **9.2** Why do you think hoteliers need to refurbish (renovate) regularly? Listen to an interview about refurbishment and check your answers.

2))) Listen again and complete the notes.

> 1 There are two types of refurbishment: [1]_____ and complete [2]_____.
> 2 Hoteliers usually refresh properties every [3]_____ to [4]_____ years.
> 3 Refreshment involves adding furniture to rooms or new [5]_____, for example, bathroom fittings or lighting, to make sure the hotel stays [6]_____.
> 4 When a hotel wants to [7]_____, or increase room rates or the number of guests, it will change complete [8]_____.
> 5 Younger customers today are attracted to either stylish [9]_____ or [10]_____.

Vocabulary

REFURBISHMENT, FURNITURE AND FITTINGS

3 What are the nouns for these verbs? Sometimes there are two: noun (thing) and noun (person).

> add   build   design   extend   innovate   upgrade

4 Complete these sentences using words associated with refurbishment. Some of the letters are given to help you.

> 1 When hoteliers [1]ref_____, they often add [2]inn_____s like in-room entertainment.
> 2 Guest rooms in boutique hotels have modern [3]fu_____: beds, bedside tables, wardrobes or closets.
> 3 Hotels in popular destinations invest a lot of money [4]up_____ing guest rooms and possibly [5]ex_____ing the hotel with new suites.
> 4 During [6]ref_____, a hotel may install high quality [7]fi_____s, such as Wi-Fi, bath-side LCD screens and larger lifts.

5 What is the Savoy famous for? Read the first paragraph of the news article and check your answers.

The Savoy reopens

The Savoy, a Fairmont Managed Hotel, has undergone one of the most ambitious restorations in British history. Established in 1889 by theatre impresario Richard D'Oyly Carte, the hotel was the first to have innovations such as en suite baths and lifts called 'ascending rooms'. Swiss hotelier, César Ritz, was the original hotel manager and Auguste Escoffier, one of the first celebrity chefs, ran the restaurant.

The Savoy closed for nearly three years during refurbishment, which involved structural upgrades and refurbishment of elegant interiors in the 1930s Art Deco style. Designer Pierre Yves Rochon has carefully restored original features including the hotel foyer.

New additions include the stately 325-square metre Royal Suite that Rochon has designed with one of the finest views of London. Thirty eight River Suites and guestrooms have been added. The Savoy has also introduced environmental technologies where possible, for example, a system that reuses the heat from kitchen appliances to preheat domestic hot water.

More than 1,000 artists and artisans have worked on its restoration. General Manager, Kieran MacDonald, commented, 'This project has not been without its difficulties … but we believe that the hotel will reclaim its position as one of the world's great hotels.'

Many celebrities have passed through its doors including Charlie Chaplin, Maria Callas, Marlene Dietrich and Frank Sinatra. The new Savoy has created nine personality suites that pay tribute to famous figures, such as the Marlene Dietrich Suite.

6 Read the rest of the article in Exercise 5. Complete the questions using the words in the box and then answer the questions.

> added   experience   implemented   open   renovated   restore   stayed   worked

1 When did the Savoy first _____?

2 What has the designer carefully _____?

3 How long did it take to _____ the hotel?

4 How many new rooms have they _____?

5 What kind of new technologies have they _____?

6 How many crafts people have _____ on the project?

7 Did the general manager _____ any difficulties?

8 Which famous guests have _____ at the Savoy?

Speaking

RENOVATION: GLAMOUR AND ELEGANCE

Pera Palace Hotel, Istanbul

Peace Hotel, Shanghai

7 Work in pairs. Student A turn to File 26, page 107. Student B turn to File 31, page 109. Take turns to ask and answer questions like those in Exercise 6 to find out about the famous hotels.

> ### RESEARCH
>
> REFURBISHMENT
> Find out about a hotel that has been restored to its original condition, or refurbished. How long did the refurbishment take? How has it changed?

PROFESSIONAL SKILLS
CHECKING OUT

Reading

EXPRESS CHECKOUT

1 Look at the stages at express checkout 1–4. Which does the guest do and which does the receptionist do? Complete the sentences with 'G' or 'R'.

1 The _____ pays by credit card when checking in and signs an express checkout card.

2 The _____ verifies the signature and checks that the credit card is valid.

3 The _____ prints out the folio/bill on the morning of departure.

4 The _____ leaves the hotel directly, leaving the room key at the front desk.

Listening

CHECKING GUESTS OUT

2 A family of three have stayed at a hotel for five nights, half-board. They pre-paid 20 percent. Check the bill and the receipts. How many items have they queried?

Hotel Havaneres restaurant

Room 309
29/8   Fresh orange juice
3x €10.50

Hotel Havaneres cafeteria

Room 309
30/8 Coffee   €10.00
31/8 Ice creams,
        drinks   €10.00
2/9   Ice creams,
        drinks   €10.00

Hotel Havaneres

Room 309
30/8   Tennis hire 3x €7.50
2/9   Tennis hire 3x €7.50

Hotel Havaneres

Room 309
1/9 Babysitter   €40.00

Hotel Havaneres

17210 Calella de Palafrugell
Costa Brava, Spain
Tel (34) 902 37 54 83
Name of guest: SUSAN MEYER
Passport No: C00008427

Room: 309
Invoice: A0001794
Reservation: 00014952
Folio: FOL-1

Date	Description	Cost	Discount	Amount in €
29/8 to 3/9	five nights, two adults HB	161.00		805.00
	five nights, one child HB	80.50 ?	-30%	281.75
29/8	Restaurant: orange juice	10.50		10.50
31/8	Restaurant: Orange juice	10.50		10.50 ?
30/8, 31/8, 2/9	Cafeteria: coffee, ice creams and drinks	10.00		30.00 ?
30/08, 2/9	Tennis hire	7.50		15.00
1/9	Babysitter one night	40.00		40.00
		Total		1,192.75 ?
		7% VAT included		
		Pre-paid		217.35
		Balance due		975.40 ?

3)))) 9.3 Listen to the family querying their bill at checkout and correct the highlighted items in the bill in Exercise 2.

4)))) Match 1–6 with a–f to complete the sentences. Listen again to check your answers.

1	That's the cost of a third	a	records for the cafeteria.
2	It's minus thirty percent,	b	due is now €964.90.
3	Let me check our	c	included in the price.
4	VAT is already	d	so we've only charged €281.75.
5	So the balance	e	new folio for you.
6	I'll print a	f	person in your room.

5)))) 9.4 Listen to the final part of the checkout. How was the guests' stay?

6)))) Listen again and <u>underline</u> the words/phrases in italics you hear.

1 *Would you like to pay / Will you be paying* with the same credit card?

2 *Could you enter / Just enter* your pin number here?

3 *Did you enjoy your stay / How was your stay* with us?

4 I'm glad to hear it. *Here's your receipt. / Do you need a receipt?*

5 Do you need *assistance / help* with your luggage?

6 Thank you for *staying with us / choosing our hotel.*

PROFESSIONAL SKILLS: CHECKING OUT

Remember to smile, maintain eye contact and address the guest(s) by name.

1 Greet the guest
Good morning, Mrs Meyer. How ¹_____ help you?
May I have your ²_____? (Ask for their name, not room number.)

2 Enquire about their stay
³_____ your stay with us? (Use open questions)
I'm glad to hear it. (after a positive comment)

3 Deal with any complaints
I ⁴_____ about that, Mrs Meyer.
⁵_____ a new folio/bill for you.

4 Offer assistance
Would you like me to book a taxi for you?
Do you need ⁶_____ with your luggage?

5 Thank the guest
Thank you ⁷_____ with us, Mrs Meyer.

---

7 Complete the useful expressions in the Professional skills box.

Speaking

CHECKING OUT

8 Work in pairs. Roleplay two hotel checkout situations. Student A turn to File 28, page 108. For the second situation, you are Student B. Turn to File 37, page 111.

Student B turn to File 9, page 103. For the second situation you are Student A. Turn to File 28, page 108.

CASE STUDY
CHOOSE A CONTRACTOR

CASE STUDY MENU

Aim: To choose a contractor for a clean-up operation after hotel refurbishment.

1 Evaluate two adverts for cleaning contractors.
2 Listen to interviews with two different contractors.
3 Explain the work required and assess the contractors' abilities for the job.
4 Confirm the agreement with the chosen contractor in writing.

Population	14 million
Location	northeast region of the USA, consists of six states; Connecticut, Maine, Massachusetts, New Hampshire, Rhode Island and Vermont.
Climate	four distinct seasons; average summer temperature is 26–29°C and 3°C in winter
Currency	US $

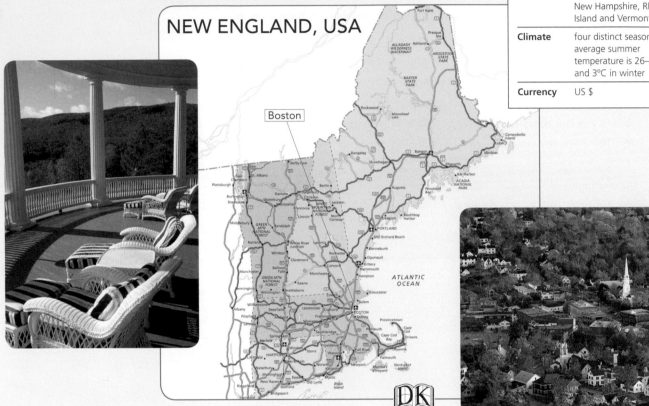

NEW ENGLAND, USA

Refurbishment clean-up

1 **Read about the Devonshire Hotel. What has happened and what needs to be done now?**

The Devonshire is a four-star hotel on the coast in New Hampshire, New England, USA. The hotel has recently refurbished its luxury rooms. It has been closed during winter but now needs a major clean-up. The new hotel manager, Emilio Méndez, is looking for a professional cleaning contractor for big jobs like window cleaning but wants to use regular staff for the suites. Emilio would like a specialist firm to do the outsourced cleaning but the hotel owners are more interested in finding a local contractor who is fast and cheap. They have already spent $600,000 on refurbishment and have gone over budget. The clean-up has to be done the last week of March – one week before the Devonshire reopens.

2 **Look at the adverts on the next page for two cleaning contractors and answer the questions. Which agency do you think …**

1 will probably be more professional?
2 will probably be more expensive?
3 doesn't have specialized equipment?
4 will probably be faster?

1 Clean & Sheen

Established in Boston in 1984, we offer cleaning services to hotels across the New England states. We specialize in:
- Pressure washing
- Carpet care
- Custom designed cleaning
- Construction clean-up

ISO 9001 registered firm

Phone 🏴 617-973-4205

2 Cleaning on Wheels

- Looking for temporary cleaners?
- Need a clean-up after renovation?

Whatever you need, we can help. We have been in the business for 15 years and offer excellent service at realistic prices. Effective and fast cleaners guaranteed!

Tel 🏴 888-253-7999

Interviewing the contractors

3 Emilio prepares to call both contractors. Look at his notes. What questions does he need to ask them?

- **Budget:** $2,500
- The hotel only has three floors but a lot of windows.
- The new restaurant has stainless steel surfaces – they should look perfect!
- Antique furniture needs environmentally safe products.
- **Time:** 3–4 days for the contractor? Staff need two days for room cleaning before the reopening.

4))) 9.5   ))) 9.6   Listen to the phone calls with each contractor and complete the table with the information.

	Clean & Sheen	Cleaning on Wheels
1 Previous experience?		.
2 Cleaning products and equipment?		
3 Cost?		
4 Time needed?		
5 Time they can visit?		

5 Emilio interviews the two contractors: Tracy from Cleaning on Wheels and Dean from Clean & Sheen. Work in pairs. Take turns to be Emilio and roleplay the interviews. Student A turn to File 29, page 108. Student B turn to File 34, page 110.

TASK

6 Decide which cleaning contractor the hotel should use and why. Compare your ideas with a partner.

7 Write an email to your chosen contractor, confirming the details for the clean-up starting next Monday. Refer to the table in Exercise 4 and confirm these points. Use the model in the Writing bank on page 99 to help you.

- start time of the clean-up
- how long it will take
- surfaces or areas that need special care
- working hours and breaks
- cost of the operation including hourly rate and any materials required

UNIT 9: KEY WORDS

carpet   design   detergent   extend   fittings   furniture   laundry   mop   remodelling   restore   sheet   stylish   toiletries   upgrade   vacuum cleaner

See DVD-ROM Mini-dictionary

10

MARKETING

UNIT MENU

Grammar: first conditional

Vocabulary: marketing and promotions, tourism trends, negotiating tactics

Professional skills: negotiating

Case study: promote a region

Reading

DESTINATION MARKETING

1 Work in pairs. Discuss the questions.

  1 What is the marketing slogan for your country or city? What idea or image of the destination is it trying to promote?

  2 Imagine the Tourism Board where you live wants to create a new slogan for your town. Brainstorm some ideas. Which one sounds the most exciting?

2 Read the text and answer the questions.

  1 How do most countries market themselves as tourist destinations?
  a internationally (to other countries)   **b** nationally (within a country)

  2 How do marketeers divide customers into different groups?

  3 What are the main elements of the marketing mix?

  4 How do organizations communicate marketing messages?

How destination marketing works

The purpose of tourism **marketing** is to **communicate** to potential customers what different destinations (countries, cities or attractions) have to offer. Most countries have a Government Tourism Administration (GTA), or National Tourist Board, which **promotes** the country abroad, often using offices across the world. Within a country, Convention and Visitors Bureaus (CVBs) – or Tourist Information Centres – are responsible for attracting visitors. Their main aim is putting 'heads in beds', whilst GTAs have the general responsibility of attracting visitors to a country.
Market researchers usually divide their potential customers into different groups or segments, according to their age, gender, lifestyle and economic status. This helps **marketeers** to develop destination marketing **campaigns** that can target specific groups or particular aspects of a destination.

If a destination has lots of outdoor facilities, the promotional material will have an active, sporty theme. However, if the destination's attraction is its cultural heritage, the material will communicate nostalgic or emotional concepts and values.
The different ways in which organizations promote their products is known as the marketing mix. This has four basic elements: product, price, **promotion** and place. 'Promotion' is about creating interest. This includes **advertising** campaigns and **sponsorship**, and using different media such as e-brochures and press releases. 'Place' refers to the channels of **distribution**: it is about getting tourism services to customers. This can be through travel agents or via social media and travel blogs on the internet, which offer an excellent way of personalizing marketing messages directly to the customer.

Vocabulary

MARKETING AND PROMOTIONS

3 Look at the words in **bold** in the text in Exercise 2 and complete the table with the words in the same family. Use a dictionary to help you.

Noun (thing)	Noun (person)	Verb
1 promotion		
2 communication		
3 market/marketing		
4 research		
5 advertisement/advertising		
6 campaign		
7 sponsorship		
8 distribution		

Listening

PROMOTING TOURISM PRODUCTS

4 What might attract tourists to South Korea?

5))) 10.1 Three tourism marketing professionals in South Korea are talking about their jobs. Make notes on who they work for and what marketing activities they do.

6))) Listen again to the speakers talking about what they do. Who does what?

1 Speaker ___: tells guests about special offers and 'upsells' in the lobby.

2 Speaker ___: hands out flyers and leaflets for a local attraction.

3 Speaker ___: brainstorms with colleagues and creates marketing slogans.

4 Speaker ___: offers discounts for business travellers.

5 Speaker ___: organizes TV commercials and outdoor advertising.

6 Speaker ___: gives tourist information about attractions to the general public.

Speaking

PROMOTING SOUTH KOREA

7 Work in pairs or groups. Brainstorm ways to promote these places or companies in South Korea. Use different marketing methods and media.

e.g. *The city hall could/might promote Seoul by putting video screens in subways in other cities.*

1 a local restaurant

2 the capital city of Seoul

3 a hotel chain

4 a low-cost airline

> **RESEARCH**
>
> MARKETING IN SOUTH KOREA
> What does South Korea have to offer? Find out how it is marketed as a tourism destination using some of these ideas: geography, capital city, main tourist attractions, food, climate and landscape. Consider promotional videos, slogans and advertisements.

TRENDS

Reading

PREDICTIONS

See INDIA

1 Which of the media below will be important in the future for marketing tourism products or services? What are the advantages and disadvantages of each? Compare your ideas with a partner.

> advertisements in print   billboard advertisements
> interactive maps   magazine   social media
> travel websites

2 Read the article about the trends that will influence future tourism and tourism marketing and match the headings a–f with the correct paragraph 1–5. One heading is not used.

a Business travel

b Destinations

c New technologies

d Food and beverage

e Outbound tourism

f Sustainable lifestyles

Tourism Trends

1 _____
Travel to the BRICs (Brazil, Russia, India and China) will grow, especially to cities like São Paolo and Rio de Janeiro. Travel to the new emerging markets, the 'Next-11' countries, including Mexico and South Korea, will increase. Inbound tourism to destinations such as Ireland, Croatia, Latvia and Lithuania will also become more popular.

2 _____
But companies will continue to ¹**cut back** and executives will have to find cheaper flights. Low-cost airlines should do well. However, hotels can continue to charge high room rates in financial centres like New York and Shanghai.

3 _____
By 2020 the number of Chinese travellers could double, depending on visa ²**restrictions**. The number of Indian travellers will probably go up by 500%. These ³**trends** mean that both India and China are going to be in the top six countries for outbound travel.

4 _____
The high profile customers of the future will be 'Lohas' (Lifestyles of Health and Sustainability): people who live, eat and travel in a healthy and ⁴**sustainable** way and are interested in spirituality and new technologies.

5 _____
Online marketing and ⁵**targeted** advertising have already replaced traditional methods. Social media is going to continue to change the way consumers make travel decisions. We will use our mobile phones as personal advisors whilst travelling, to make online bookings, open hotel doors and use as 'mobile ⁶**wallets**' for payment.

3 Choose the correct definition for the words in **bold** in the text.

1 a increase the amount of something   **b** reduce the amount of something

2 a application forms   **b** rules or laws that limit you

3 a doing something that other people copy   **b** the way a situation is changing

4 a safe for the environment   **b** dangerous for the environment

5 a with an effect on a particular group   **b** something you try to achieve

6 a small flat case for money and bank cards   **b** large leather case for documents

4 Which trends have/haven't come true? Which new technologies do you use to make your travel decisions?

GRAMMAR: FIRST CONDITIONAL

Use the **first conditional** to talk about real possibilities in the present or future.

Use (**If** + present simple) + (**will** + infinitive).
Use contractions (**'ll** and **won't**) when speaking.
*If a traveller **has** a positive experience, she**'ll write** a review on the internet.*

Use the adverb **probably** when you are less sure. Note the word order.
*If we use more digital media, print media **will probably/probably won't** disappear.*

Sometimes you can use **when** instead of *if.*
*Will you confirm your booking please **when** you receive the information?*

See Grammar reference, page 116.

5 Six travel experts are making predictions about future travel trends. Work in pairs. What do you predict they will say about the future of the following?

1 Wi-Fi charges in hotels
2 airline charges
3 travel for singles
4 travel agents
5 general packages
6 online information videos

6))) **10.2** Listen to the travel experts' predictions and compare them with your ideas in Exercise 5.

7))) Study the Grammar box and complete the first conditional sentences with the correct form of the verbs in brackets. Listen again and check your answers.

1 If luxury hotels continue to [1]_____ (charge) ten dollars for Wi-Fi, they [2]____ (lose) guests, especially business guests.

2 If low-cost carriers [3]____ (charge) for using the restroom or toilet on flights, other airlines [4]____ probably [5]____ (do) the same.

3 I think if solo travel [6]____ (become) more popular, cruises and hotels [7]____ (stop) charging single supplements.

4 People [8]____ (go back) to using travel agents if there [9]____ (be) too much information online.

5 If consumers [10]____ (have) more specific interests, tourism organizations [11]____ (not be able) to sell general packages.

Speaking

CONDITIONAL CHAINS

8))) **10.3** How do you think this 'conditional chain' continues? Work in pairs. Try to add at least FOUR more sentences. Then listen and write down the eight sentences you hear.

e.g. If there is a natural disaster, the airports will close.   If the airports close, airlines will …   If airlines …, passengers …

9 Work in pairs. Use the ideas 1–3 to start conditional chains. Take turns to add sentences. Try to keep the chain going as long as possible.

1 If a traveller has a negative holiday experience, …

2 If tourist boards don't have creative marketing campaigns, …

3 If the number of mid-priced hotels increases, …

BRAZIL

BRAZILIAN INFORMATION BUREAU
511 FIFTH AVENUE · NEW YORK

PROFESSIONAL SKILLS
NEGOTIATING

Reading

NEGOTIATING TACTICS

1 **Look at the negotiation tactics below. Tick (✓) the tactics you think are a bad idea. Compare your ideas with a partner.**

1 _____ prepare before you negotiate

2 _____ take notes during the negotiation

3 _____ be the first to offer a concession

4 _____ start with a very high/low price

5 _____ study people's body language

6 _____ don't show your emotions

7 _____ pretend you're not interested

8 _____ be sociable when necessary

2 **Read the negotiation tips. Which of the tactics in Exercise 1 are mentioned?**

Seven tips for negotiating

• Prepare as much as possible before a negotiation: find out as much as you can about your partner, their organization and culture. Decide what concessions you are prepared to make before you start the negotiation.

• Always be polite and respectful, especially when talking to people in authority.

• Listen carefully and make notes. Try not to be the first to make an offer, or a concession, e.g. a discount.

• Be aware of body language, e.g. people who agree with you often mirror or copy your movements and gestures. Watch out for negative body language, such as crossing arms, turning away from you or lack of eye contact.

• Negotiations can seem very slow in some cultures, especially for people from Anglo-American or German cultures. Other people's attitudes to punctuality, time and interruptions may be very different from yours.

• Hospitality is very important in many countries. Use these opportunities, such as business lunches to get to know your business partners better.

• The best negotiations offer a 'win-win' solution for both parties. But sometimes you 'walk away' (politely) from a negotiation if you think there won't be a positive outcome for you and your organization. You will be more successful if you are patient, friendly and flexible.

Listening

NEGOTIATIONS

3))) 10.4 **Listen to a tourist bargaining over the price of a Turkish carpet in the bazaar in Istanbul, Turkey. Tick (✓) the correct outcome.**

1 _____ The carpet dealer sells the carpet for 250 Turkish lira (TRY).

2 _____ The man negotiates 200 TRY for a carpet and two cushions.

3 _____ The woman buys a carpet and a bag for 220 TRY.

4 Which negotiating tactics from Exercise 1 does the carpet dealer use? Which does the tourist use?

5))) 10.5   ))) 10.6   Listen to two more negotiations and answer the questions.

1 What is Vassili's new job in Bodrum?

2 What will his salary and benefits be?

3 What other benefits does he try to negotiate for?

4 How many sun loungers and parasols does the tourist first ask for?

5 How many loungers does the attendant offer and for what price?

6 What is the final price?

PROFESSIONAL SKILLS: NEGOTIATING

1 Saying 'no'
Sorry, this area is reserved for guests only.
Sorry, no. This area is ¹_____.

2 Reacting to someone walking away
Wait a minute. Perhaps I ²_____ *a special offer.*
Listen, I'm sure we can come to an agreement.

3 Talking about possibilities
If there are four of you, you'll have to pay for two umbrellas.
If you want four loungers, ³_____ *two umbrellas.*

4 Offering a concession
Four loungers for the price of three, and I ⁴_____ *for the second umbrella.*
I can give you a 20% discount.

5 Asking for a response
So that's only 14 TRY. ⁵_____ *that sound?*
What if I give it to you for 14 lira?

6 Building relationships
I'll make you a ⁶_____ *because you're from Hotel Ephesus.*
Enjoy your holiday/stay/vacation!

---

6))) 10.6   Listen again and complete the negotiating expressions 1–6 in the Professional skills box. Check your answers in audio script 10.6 on page 128.

7 Match phrases 1–5 with phrases a–e to complete the negotiating expressions.

1 If you don't have TRY,

2 Before you go, take a look at

3 If you tell your friends about this restaurant,

4 What if you upgrade to the suite?

5 150 TRY for the rooms? Sorry,

a we'll give them a 10 percent discount.

b You'll be more comfortable and it's only 220 TRY.

c we'll accept other currencies.

d but the special offer finished last week.

e these souvenirs – they're half price.

Speaking

NEGOTIATIONS

8 Work in pairs. Student A turn to File 30, page 108. Student B turn to File 35, page 110. Roleplay two negotiations.

CASE STUDY PROMOTE A REGION

Aim: To create a commercial to promote tourism in Isan, Thailand.

1 Listen to and complete information about Thailand and Isan.

2 Exchange information about the Isan region.

3 Decide on key tourism values for promoting Isan and which segments to target.

4 Write the storyboard or script and slogan for a TV or radio commercial.

Thailand and the Isan region

1  **10.7** **Listen to an extract from a programme about Thailand and the Isan region. Answer the questions.**

1 What two things do tourists come to Thailand for?

2 In which part of Thailand is the Isan region?

3 What is special about Isan? How is it different from other parts of Thailand?

Population	66,700,000
Capital and major airport	Bangkok
Currency	Thai baht
Major languages	Thai
Climate	the Thai year depends on the monsoons and its three seasons: wet, cool and hot
Main attractions	nightlife in Bangkok, festivals, trekking, elephant riding, historic sites, tropical islands and Thai food

2 **)))** **Complete the text about the Isan region with appropriate adjectives. Listen again to check your answers. You can also look at audio script 10.7 on page 128.**

Isan region – Thailand

The northeast of Thailand, known as Isan, has a(n) ¹_____, unique culture. Isan is situated on the Khorat plateau, and the Mekong river borders this part of Thailand with Laos. It is a region ²_____ by mass tourism and is ideal for travellers looking for a(n) ³_____ travel experience. If you travel in the northeast, you will discover the ⁴_____ and friendly Isan people, and their ⁵_____ culture and historic heritage. Isan also has ⁶_____ landscapes, ⁷_____ boxing and Isan food, ⁸_____ all over Thailand for its ⁹_____ rice and chillies. And, sweet mangoes served with coconut cream!

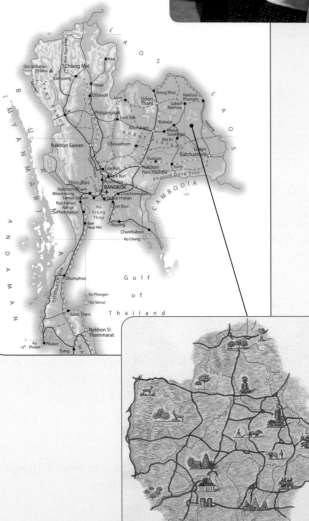

THAILAND

ISAN

Tourism in Isan

3 Work in pairs. Student A, look at the information below. Student B turn to File 32, page 109. Take turns to ask and answer questions to find out more information about Isan.

1 the best times to visit Isan and Thailand
2 value for money
3 how Isan is different
4 the main attractions in Isan
5 accommodation in Isan
6 the people of Isan

Tourism in Thailand

Thailand is one of the world's best value destinations, although there has been increased competition since Laos, Cambodia and Vietnam opened up to international tourism in the 1980s. **The weather:** in the north, the rainy season is from May to November, the cool season is the best time to visit (November to February); the hot season is March to May.

Isan region

The main city is Khorat. The Mekong River valley separates the region from its neighbour, Laos. Most of its people are ethnically Lao and are known for their hospitality. Isan has many national parks for trekking.

Khon Kaen: The town of Khon Kaen in the centre of Isan was once a quiet place but it has become a busy university town. There are modern hotels and shops next to traditional streets and market places.

Ubon Ratchathani: Ubon Province in the east of the Mekong river valley has many natural attractions: ancient cave drawings, strange rock formations and beautiful waterfalls, such as the Than Thip Falls near Sangkhom. This waterfall is 30 m high and in the rainy season there's a large pool for swimming. The province is popular with backpackers who stay in bamboo huts by the river. In July, the town of Ubon holds a spectacular candle festival when villagers make enormous candles.

TASK

4 Work in groups. Hold a meeting to discuss how you can market Isan to your country.

1 Choose three of the most important values for your marketing campaign. Use ideas from the box and your own.
2 Consider the different market segments. Which one(s) will you target?
3 What features and attractions in Isan will your campaign focus on?

> **Tourism values**
>
> adventure activities   family holidays   friendly people   good food
> Khmer history and culture   luxury resorts   natural beauty   nightlife   river life
> safety and security   solo travel   sustainable tourism   transport   unspoilt beaches
> value for money   warm weather

Market segments

1 High income professionals with little time
2 Families with children
3 Young people on a low budget
4 'Baby boomers' – older people with time and money

5 Work in small groups. Create a ONE- to TWO-minute TV or radio commercial to promote Isan in your country.

1 Brainstorm different ideas and then choose the best one.
2 Write up a storyboard or script. Include a description of the characters and setting with ideas for music or sound effects.
3 The commercial should reflect three tourism values and target specific market segments.
4 Give your campaign a slogan.

> **UNIT 10: KEY WORDS**
>
> advertisement   bargain
> campaign   commercial
> discount   e-brochure   flyer
> market research/segment
> marketeer   negotiation
> promote   promotion   slogan
> social media   print
> **See DVD-ROM Mini-dictionary**

Describing dishes

1 Complete the text on Turkish food with the correct option in 1–12.

Turkish ¹_____ on the Mediterranean and Aegean coasts is known for its fresh fruit, vegetables and fish. In Turkey, a ²_____ often begins with sharing a selection of ³_____ or starters known as mezes. In basic *meyhane* (the traditional restaurants in Turkey and Iran), diners eat ⁴_____, cheese and ⁵_____ of melon served with cream cheese. More expensive, upmarket restaurants offer a wide choice of vegetable dishes ⁶_____ at room temperature: green beans with tomato ⁷_____, stuffed vine leaves, or artichokes ⁸_____ olive oil and salads, typically ⁹_____with tomato, red onion and cucumber. Mezes can also include hot ¹⁰_____, such as borek, which are cheese pastries, or shellfish and ¹¹_____, such as fried mussels and squid. Appetizers are ¹²_____ with bread.

1 chefs / cuisine / cook / restaurant
2 food / meat / portion / meal
3 order / main courses / appetizers / drinks
4 breakfasts / desserts / olives / grilled
5 juices / slices / bits / lots
6 coated / homemade / served / marinated
7 cream / fresh / homemade / sauce
8 cooked in / stuffed with / baked in / made with
9 boiled / made / roasted / came
10 dishes / napkins / side orders / diets
11 set menu / prawns / fruit / seafood
12 eaten / taken / drank / had

Quantifiers

2 Circle the correct quantifiers in italics.

1 The hotel isn't catering for *a lot of / much* wedding guests at this event – about 125.

2 How *many / much* guests have special dietary needs?

3 We've taken on *some / any* new kitchen staff – a sous chef and two prep cooks.

4 The waiting staff are professional here but they don't speak *much / many* English.

5 Can you take *some / any* wine glasses from table five?

6 I'd like *a / an* omelette, and could you bring me *a / the* clean knife, please?

7 The lamb comes with *– / a* French fries, or *– / a* rice.

8 So that's two main courses with a salad on the side. *Something / Anything* else?

9 Would you like *much / some* coffee with your desserts?

10 Customers don't usually leave *a / –* large tip in my country.

Future forms

3 Which sentence is incorrect?

1
a If you're interested in nature and wildlife, you'll love Costa Rica.
b If you're interested in nature and wildlife, you're going to love Costa Rica.
c If you're interested in nature and wildlife, you're loving Costa Rica.

2
a The bus tour'll leave tomorrow at 8.30 a.m.
b The bus tour going to leave tomorrow at 8.30 a.m.
c The bus tour's leaving tomorrow at 8.30 a.m.

3
a They won't go glacier trekking this week.
b They aren't going to glacier trekking this week.
c They aren't going glacier trekking this week.

4
a We will take the flightseeing tour on day two?
b Are we going to take the flightseeing tour on day two?
c Are we taking the flightseeing tour on day two?

5
a I hope there won't be any mosquitoes in the jungle lodge.
b I hope there aren't going to be any mosquitoes in the jungle lodge.
c I hope there aren't being any mosquitoes in the jungle lodge.

Presentations

4 Put the notes from Tamsin's presentation in the correct order. Then write the correct function for 1–6: visuals (V), starting (S) or ending (E).

1 show / to / I'd like / amazing / you a / video / of this / tour.

2 going to / about Auckland / Hello I'm / Tamsin and / in New Zealand. / I'm / tell you

3 be / Right, / take any / I'll / questions now. / happy to

4 you ever / Queenstown? / heard of / capital. / Have / adventure / It's our

5 if you / Auckland is / So, / outdoor activities, / for you! / love

6 see, / is enormous. / As you / the geographical / of our country / can / diversity

Obligation

5 Complete the travel information for airline passengers in China with the verbs of obligation in the box. Some verbs may be used more than once.

> are allowed   don't have to   has   is allowed
> must   mustn't   should   shouldn't

Flight information – China

For international flights passengers ¹_____ check in at least two hours before departure. For domestic flights passengers ²_____ really check in one and a half hours before departure but in fact, passengers often don't arrive that early. Most passengers ³_____ up to 20 kg of luggage. An airline passenger ⁴_____ one additional item of hand luggage weighing up to 5 kg. But a passenger who has excess baggage ⁵_____ to pay more. You ⁶_____ pay extra for the airport tax – it is included in the price of the ticket.
Not all ticket offices and travel agents in China accept credit cards, so travellers ⁷_____ be prepared to pay in cash. Visitors ⁸_____ show their passports when purchasing tickets. It is usual to ask for a reduction on official fares, and whatever price is first offered, travellers ⁹_____ always ask for a discount. Children over the age of 12 ¹⁰_____ pay the adult fare but younger children ¹¹_____ be charged the full price. Ticket prices are more expensive between June and September and during Chinese holidays: the Spring Festival (or Chinese New Year), and the May and October holiday periods.
On arrival, visitors ¹²_____ complete a form for health, immigration and customs as part of Chinese regulations.

Air travel

6 Read the definitions and write the words associated with air travel to complete the crossword.

Across

4 place where passengers arrive in an airport
6 area where passengers go just before the plane leaves
8 journey on a plane, or a plane making a particular journey
9 relaxed and not worried, angry or upset
10 period of time when you have to wait for something to happen

Down

1 area in an airport where passengers board an airplane
2 when a plane moves off the ground and into the air
3 when a plane moves down until it is safely on the ground
5 screening checkpoint where passengers must pass before boarding a plane
7 all of a traveller's personal belongings – checked or unchecked

Present perfect

7 A reporter is asking a hotel manager about the refurbishment of a hotel in Los Angeles. Put the verbs in brackets in the present perfect tense. Use contractions where possible.

R = Reporter, H = Hotel Manager

R: How many new guest rooms ¹_____ (you/add)?

H: We ²_____ (extend) ten rooms and remodelled the five suites.

R: What kind of new fittings ³_____ (you/install)?

H: We've installed new lighting, in-room entertainment and luxury bathroom fittings.

R: ⁴_____ (there/be) any other changes?

H: Yes, the architect ⁵_____ (redesign) the restaurant and café. These have a Hollywood theme. And we ⁶_____ (replace) the revolving doors in the lobby, which were too small, and the lifts have also been ⁷_____ (make) bigger.

R: ⁸_____ (you/renovate) any original features?

H: Yes, we have. The façade of the building has been ⁹_____ (restore). The builders removed the old paint so it has its original colour.

R: Anything else?

H: The designer ¹⁰_____ (buy) some Art Deco furniture and put photographs of our famous guests in the suites. The designer ¹¹_____ (also/put) on display some valuable objects, such as an old film script and a 1930s dress.

R: ¹²_____ (you/finish) the refurbishment yet?

H: No, not yet. We are still cleaning the public areas. But we will reopen in time for the film festival next week.

Hotel checkout

8 Complete the checkout conversation between a front desk agent and a guest.

F = Front Desk Agent, G = Guest

F: How can I ¹h_____ you?

G: I'd like to check out, please.

F: It's Mr Chen, isn't it?

G: Yes. I have a copy of the ²b_____ here. But I'm afraid I don't have my glasses on me. Could you tell me what these forty dollars are for?

F: That's the ³l_____ charge for washing and ironing two shirts.

G: Ah, yes. And what about the twenty dollar charge?

F: Let me check our ⁴r_____. That's for room service.

G: But I didn't ask for any room service.

F: I'll just ⁵c_____. Yes, there seems to have been a ⁶m_____ here. I'm very ⁷s_____ about that. So the ⁸b_____ due is now ninety-five dollars. Are you ⁹p_____ by credit card?

G: Yes, please.

F: Have you ¹⁰e_____ your stay, Mr Chen?

G: Yes, I loved the gym and spa.

F: Glad to hear it. And do you need ¹¹a_____ with your luggage?

G: No, I'm fine, thanks.

F: Thank you for ¹²s_____ with us and we hope to see you again soon!

Tourism marketing

9 Complete the sentences about tourism marketing using the correct form of the word in brackets.

1 Tourism marketing involves creating and planning the price, ¹_____ (promote) and ²_____ (distribute) of tourism products and services.

2 Dividing the population into different market ³_____ (segment) means tourism organizations can offer different types of ⁴_____ (production) or services to different groups.

3 An effective ⁵_____ (market) campaign helps to ⁶_____ (attraction) visitors to a destination using different media: print, TV, radio and online social media.

4 The internet is the tool that is most used to ⁷_____ (researcher) travel: people often consult social media sites, user reviews and forums before booking.

5 ⁸_____ (sponsor) is when organizations or individuals give money to pay for a sports, arts or training events in exchange for ⁹_____ (advert) or attracting public attention.

6 A weak or confusing marketing campaign means a destination isn't ¹⁰_____ (promote) effectively.

Making recommendations

10 Complete a travel agent's recommendations. Put the verb in brackets in the first conditional. Use contractions where possible.

1 If you ¹_____ (visit) Salzburg in Austria, you ²_____ (see) Mozart's house in the Mozarteum.

2 If you ³_____ (go) to the North Island in New Zealand, you ⁴_____ (not/see) any glaciers.

3 If he ⁵_____ (go) shopping in the Grand Bazaar in Istanbul, he ⁶_____ (always/should/bargain) prices.

4 If she ⁷_____ (visit) Surin in January, she ⁸_____ (not/see) the Elephant Round-up that takes place in November.

5 He ⁹_____ (love) the jungle tour when he ¹⁰_____ (be) in Costa Rica.

6 When you ¹¹_____ (be) in Poland in the summer, you ¹²_____ (love) swimming in its many lakes.

Hotel refurbishment

11 Put the words/phrases associated with hotel refurbishment in the box with the correct heading 1–3.

> anti-theft clothes hangers   armchair   bath-side LCD screen   bedside table
> closet   decorate   desk   drawers   electronic blinds   lighting   refresh
> remodelling   renovation   shower screen   upgrade

1 Refurbishment   2 Furniture   3 Fittings

Negotiating

12 Match phrases 1–6 with a–f to complete the conditional sentences about what tourism professionals say when negotiating.

1 If you dine between 6 p.m. and 7 p.m., ___

2 It'll only cost an extra 25 dollars ___

3 10,000 pounds for the contract? I'm sorry but ___

4 If you report to me at 8 a.m., ___

5 We'll pay for you to fly home once a year ___

6 If you work hard and are willing to learn, ___

a if you accept this job.

b I'll introduce you to the other staff.

c we'll give you free drinks with your meal.

d we can't do business with you this time.

e we'll be happy to promote you next year.

f if you upgrade to the executive suite.

WRITING BANK

Covering letters and CVs

LETTER FOR A SPECULATIVE APPLICATION

Always include a covering letter when you send a job application. It should be between three to five short paragraphs in length.

Alessia Belmonte
Via Michelangelo, 18
00198 Rome
Italy
Tel. 39 06 85 376 8224

Director of Human Resources

Mercurio Tours

Dear Sir/Madam,

Are you looking for an experienced tour guide with excellent communication skills who speaks three languages? I am writing to your tour company because I am very interested in working for *Mercurio Tours*. I have read many positive recommendations for your excellent tours. ●

At the moment I am studying for a postgraduate diploma in Tourism at the University of Rome. I have two years' experience of working as a tour guide for local school groups. I also have a degree in History and specialist knowledge of Rome and Italy's historic sites. Please find enclosed a copy of my CV for your interest. ●

I believe I will be a valuable asset to your company because I am outgoing, communicative and organized. My tutor says I am always enthusiastic and have good leadership skills. ●

As you can see from my CV, I can drive and speak both Italian and English fluently. In addition, I am currently learning Chinese.

Please do not hesitate to contact me regarding a possible interview if you would like to discuss my experience in more detail. I look forward to hearing from you. ●

Yours faithfully,

Alessia Belmonte ●

Alessia Belmonte

> Personalize the letter: refer to the company name in the first paragraph.

> Briefly describe your qualifications and/or experience. Refer to your CV.

> Explain why the organization should hire you: describe your key qualities and skills.

> Refer to a job interview in the final paragraph.

> Sign the letter if you are sending it by post.

EMAIL SENDING A COVERING LETTER AND CV – ADVERTISED VACANCY

You can either write your covering letter in the body of an email or send it as an attachment. However, you shouldn't write your CV in the body of the email because managers usually want to add it to a database.

Ref: 304/B Marketing and sales ●

Dear Sir/Madam,

I am very interested in your online advertisement in *T&T Jobs* and I would like to apply for the above position. ● Please find attached a copy of my covering letter and CV.

If you need any more information, do not hesitate to contact me. I look forward to hearing from you regarding a possible interview.

Best regards,

Anthony Chan

> Refer to the reference number with an advertised vacancy.

> Mention where you saw the advertisement when applying for an advertised job position.

Writing a CV

A CV is a short document that lists your education and jobs, which you send to employers when you are looking for a job. The way you organize your CV varies from country to country, and depends on your age and experience, the type of company and the job you are applying for. Here are some guidelines:

Length: A CV is usually no more than two pages if it is for an advertised vacancy (job position). It is no more than one page if it is a speculative application (with no advertised vacancy), or if you don't have much experience.

Personal details: Include your name in full, address, telephone number(s) and email address, etc. at the top.

Profile: Some companies like candidates to include a profile statement at the start of their CV. This is a summary of your key skills and strengths, and shouldn't be more than 100 words, e.g. *I am a qualified front desk clerk with two years' experience working for an international hotel chain …*

Education and qualifications and professional/ work experience: If you are a younger candidate without much work experience, list your education first. You can do this in chronological order but it is more usual to list it in reverse chronological order with the most recent place of study or job position first, e.g. *Guide at the National Art Museum, 20th December to present.* If you have a lot of experience, then list your experience first and be selective – don't include jobs you only did for a short time, e.g. *Cloakroom attendant, 199 Dance Club (3 days).*

Dates: Include accurate dates for work experience and education, e.g. *ABC Tourism School, September 2000– June 2013.*

Additional training: This section includes any other relevant courses you have done, e.g. *Sales skills for front desk staff (20 hours).*

Skills-based CV: If you have worked in different sectors, you can also organize your CV according to the sector with the most relevant one first, or list your key skills at the start.

Languages: Include your language skills, mention any official certificates you have and describe your level, e.g. *elementary* or *basic, intermediate, advanced, fluent.*

Computer/IT skills: List the computer programmes, databases, etc. you know how to use.

Additional information: e.g. *I have a clean driving licence.*

Hobbies and interests: These are usually listed at the end. Mention if you have been a member of a club or organization where you learnt useful skills, e.g. *President of the basketball club at college/ university.*

Referees: These are people in a position of authority who know you well and will give you a positive recommendation. If you include the names of two referees, also give their phone numbers and (email) addresses but make sure you check with them first! Many applicants often write: *References and certificates available upon request.*

Application forms: Some large companies and organizations will often ask you to complete their own application form instead of sending your CV. Complete this as fully as possible.

Photo: Many companies prefer job applicants to include a photo in their CV but this is a personal choice.

Never lie in your CV! This will only cause you problems at the interview or on your first day of work.

Check your CV: Ask a friend, teacher or colleague to check your CV and covering letter before you send it. What impression do they give? Would they employ you? Why (not)?

USEFUL EXPRESSIONS FOR COVERING LETTERS

I am writing to enquire whether you have a vacancy in your company for a tour guide.

I attach a copy of my CV (for your consideration).

Please find attached a copy of my CV (for your interest).

My current responsibilities include …

As you will see from my CV, I …

Communication and organizational skills are my main strengths.

I consider myself hard working and enthusiastic, and I enjoy working in a team.

I have many transferable skills from my previous job position, such as …

I am willing to learn new skills.

I am very interested in being part of your company/organization.

I feel that I could make a significant contribution to your team.

Formal business letter

The content of a formal letter should be as short and clear as possible. Make sure your letter is formal and polite in style and use short, easy-to-read, sentences and paragraphs with one main point in each paragraph. Remember not to use informal language or contractions and don't forget to read through what you have written before you send it to check your grammar, spelling and punctuation. Mistakes create a bad impression.

Salutations:
- *Dear Sir or Madam* or *Dear Sir/Madam* (when you are writing to a company or organization, and you don't know if you are writing to a man or woman)
- *Dear title + surname* or *Dear title + first name + surname* (when you know the person's name)

Endings:
- When you don't know the person's name, end the letter *Yours faithfully*.
- When you use the name of the person, end the letter *Yours sincerely*.

TopNotch International Hotels
60–66 Park Avenue
London SW3 8RH
T: +44 (0) 207 780 5700
tnreservations@topnotch.com
www.topnothcint.com

Use your company's or organization's letterhead. Put the address, phone number, email address, website and other contact details in the top, right-hand corner.

Patricia Montero
Executive Assistant
Sirena Engineering
6773 Marine Drive
North Miami, Florida
USA 33160

Put the name and address of the person you are writing to on the left-hand side of the letter. This information can be opposite or below your address. Include his/her position (if known).

14 January 2014

Dear Ms Montero,

Reservation: Sirena Engineering 3 May–10 May 2014

Put the subject of the letter (and reference number, when appropriate) below the salutation in bold or underlined to make it easier for the reader to see what you are writing about.

In reference to our telephone call today, I am pleased to confirm your company's booking with our hotel. The details are as follows:

Reservation number: TN03459B

Arrival date: 3 May 2014   Departure date: 10 May 2014

Number of guests: 20

Accommodation: four junior suites and two executive suites

Rate per night: junior suite £275, executive suite £350 (excluding taxes)

Check-in: 2.00 p.m.   Checkout: 12.00 p.m.

You also booked a meeting room and catering. Please find attached the rates for the conference facilities and payment details.

If you have any queries or need to make any changes to this booking, please contact me or one of our reservations assistants at the telephone number or email above.

Thank you for choosing TopNotch International.

Yours sincerely,

Adam Harper

Adam Harper
Reservations Manager
TopNotch International London

Put the reason for writing in the first paragraph. Give more details in the middle paragraphs.

The date can be on the left or right hand side, below the address of the recipient. In British English the date order is 14 January 2014 (day/month/year). American English puts the month first, e.g. January 14 or 1/14/2014. Write the month in words to avoid confusion.

Tell the reader what action you would like them to take in the final paragraphs. Thank the reader, if appropriate.

Sign your name by hand and type your full name and position under the signature.

Emails

Emails are often shorter and less formal than letters. However, in business writing it is usual to write formal emails to people you don't know. As for formal letters, you should use simple language and short easy-to-read sentences and paragraphs. Include detailed information as attachments, not in the body of the email. Emails are quicker to write than letters but it is easy to make a mistake when writing quickly, so don't forget to check all the details, e.g. names, dates, times, prices, as well as your spelling and grammar, before sending an email message.

Salutations:
- When writing to several people, you can use *Dear all* or *Hello everyone*.
- In less formal emails, *Hello* and *Hi* are common greetings.

Endings:
- Use *Best wishes*, *Best regards*, *Kind regards* or simply, *Regards*.

RESPONDING TO COMPLAINTS

From:	Francoise Dupree
To:	Armand Fuller
Subject:	Guest Evaluation

Use the subject line to indicate to the reader what you are writing about.

Dear Mr Fuller,

Thank you for completing the guest evaluation form during your stay at our hotel last week. We welcome feedback from our guests. It is an opportunity to improve the quality of the guest experience.

Start by thanking the client if appropriate.

I am very sorry to hear that your bathroom was not very clean. Thank you for bringing this matter to our attention. That is not the usual standard of our hotel and we are investigating the situation.

Please also accept my apologies for the noise you heard from the housekeepers in the early hours of the morning. It is never pleasant to have a disturbed night's sleep. Unfortunately, your room was next to their room on that floor, and our staff did not know that the noise was disturbing you.

When responding to a complaint, remember to apologize, e.g. *I apologize for*, *I am very sorry for*, *I am very sorry to hear that …*, *Please also accept my apologies for …* and show empathy for your customer's situation.

Once again, I apologize for the inconvenience caused during your stay with us. I hope you will come back soon and give us an opportunity to restore your confidence in our hotel.

Best regards,

Francoise Dupree

Duty Manager

Marcini Hotel

CONFIRMING A BOOKING

From:	Valentina Vazquez
To:	Kichi Hayashi
Subject:	Your booking

Use the subject line to indicate to the reader what you are writing about.

Dear Mr Kichi Hayashi,

Thank you for booking with Val's Vacations. I am writing to confirm the details of your booking to Argentina for eight nights.Your travel dates are from 23 June to 1 July. Your package tour includes flights for two persons and half–board accommodation in four star hotels.

Please find attached your flight information with Amazing Airlines and details of your hotels, airport transfers and tour information.

The total cost of your booking is (total cost of booking). We accept payment by credit card or bank transfer. Please don't hesitate to contact me if you have any questions.

In the last paragraph, invite the customer to contact you if they have any questions.

Regards,

Valentina Vazquez

Travel specialist

Val's Vacations

Menus

Use a good dictionary to check your translations, vocabulary and spelling. Mistakes create a bad impression.

Use adjectives to make the dish sound more appetizing. Research shows that more descriptive menus can increase sales. Four typical descriptions are:

a Geographical, e.g. Tex-Mex salad, Thai grilled beef

b Nostalgic, e.g. Grandma's apple pie, classic Sunday roast

c Sensory, e.g. creamy chocolate mousse, spicy chicken curry

d Brand names

Use logos to indicate if a dish is suitable for special diets, e.g. vegetarian or is a healthy option.

Donna's Bistro

Starters/Appetizers

French onion soup
Delicious homemade soup made with beef and onions – comes with Swiss cheese and breadcrumbs.

Seafood special
Fresh white fish, prawns and mussels, cooked in olive oil and onions.

Ⓥ Tasty baked camembert
Coated in breadcrumbs and served with salad.

Main courses

Thai grilled beef salad
Tender pieces of beef grilled to perfection and served with salad.

Spicy barbeque chicken
Marinated in lemon juice, chilli, olive oil and garlic, and then barbequed.

Donna's veggie burger
Ⓥ Donna's classic homemade veggie burger, served with chips or salad.

Desserts

Traditional summer pudding
Made with blackberries, raspberries and strawberries, and served with cream.

Creamy chocolate mousse
Chocolate-lovers' paradise!

Fresh fruit salad
Pineapple, peach, orange, banana, kiwi and strawberry.

Tour programme or itinerary

Give your tour a name.

Say what is or isn't included in the programme.

Give an overview or summary of the tour.

Grizzly Bear Tours

All transfers are included	Sightseeing excursions with guides
• flights between Vancouver and Campbell River • floatplane between Campbell River and Knight Inlet • transfers between Campbell River airport and your lodge	• bear viewing tour • scenic boat ride • hiking in Kwalate river valley • eagle viewing tour • river cruise

The total cost and the costs of any optional extras should be clearly marked.

Total cost, four days/three nights:
CAD $2,250 per person sharing a double room, $3,125 for single occupancy

Be enthusiastic about the tour and add details to make it more interesting.

DAY 1 – Vancouver to Campbell River
3 p.m.: One-hour flight from Vancouver International Airport to Campbell River, the salmon fishing capital of the world!
5 p.m.: Check in at hotel in Campbell River – enjoy some free time exploring the town. Walk along Discovery Pier with magnificent views of Quadra Island and the mountains of British Columbia.
8 p.m.: Meet the other tour participants at dinner (*optional, $28 per head).

State clearly if the tours, activities and excursions are with (or without) guides.

DAY 2 – Grizzly bear viewing

DAY 3 – Grizzly bear viewing and scenic boat ride

Schedule some free time and some time for socializing.

DAY 4 – Campbell River to Vancouver
9 a.m.: A final opportunity to see the bears!
11 a.m.: Depart for the floatplane flight to Campbell River. Transfer to the airport for flight to Vancouver International Airport.

All other meals are included and cooked with local ingredients.

PAIRWORK FILES

File 1, unit 1, page 8

1 France	**3** China	**5** Italy
2 the USA	**4** Spain	**6** the UK

File 2, unit 1, page 10

The Great USA Quiz answers:

1 a Canada

2 c $3,500

3 b 16 nights

4 c Times Square, New York

5 c 37 million

6 The Grand Canyon in Arizona

7 vacation – holiday, cab – taxi, elevator – lift, restroom – toilet

8 a the fourth Thursday in November

File 3, unit 1, page 12

1 Dates

Use ordinal numbers, e.g. *first, second, third, fourth, fifth, sixth* for dates.

In American English, say the month first, then the date.

10/12/20 = October twelfth 2020
12/10/20 = December tenth 2020

In British English, say the date first, then the month.

12/10/20 = the twelfth of October 2020
10/12/20 = the tenth of December 2020

In writing, it isn't necessary to write the ordinal number but it can make dates clearer.

26 January 2020 √   26th January 2020 √

2 Times

Either use *o'clock, (a) quarter, half* with *past* and *to*.

It's eight o'clock, five past eight, (a) quarter past eight, twenty past eight, half past eight, twenty to nine, (a) quarter to nine, etc.

Or say the times as numbers.

It's nine (a.m./p.m.), nine fifteen, nine twenty, nine thirty, nine thirty-five, nine forty-five, nine fifty-five, etc.

File 4, unit 1, page 13

STUDENT A

Booking 1

You are the head waiter at a top hotel restaurant in Ottawa, Canada. Think of a name for the restaurant.

- Answer the phone and take the details for a booking. There are two sittings (8 p.m. and 10 p.m.).

- The restaurant is part of a group but the other thematic restaurants – an Italian and an Indian restaurant – are closed at the moment.

- Remember to ask for the caller's details: name and phone number.

Booking 2
You would like to book 15 seats for the Australian Open in Melbourne this January for some clients of your company.

- Phone to reserve your seats and ask if there is a discount for group bookings – it isn't possible to book more than seven tickets online.

- Check the ticket prices – nothing too expensive – and if the booking fee is included.

- Be prepared to spell your name and give a credit card number, your phone number and your email address.

File 5, unit 1, page 15

STUDENT A

You are a travel consultant at CSAM Travel. Mark phones you to confirm his booking details. Ask about these details and take notes during your conversation so that you can give him the total cost at the end.

1 Mark's travel dates.

2 The following are included in the price of the packages:

- Aeromexico return flights, departing from Mexico City, arriving in Lima or Cusco

- internal flights to the Amazon for jungle tours

- English-speaking guides, all transfers, entrance tickets, accommodation and meals (breakfast and dinner)

3 The Inca Trail trekking tours are all with a guide:

- Peru Special: three days, challenging physical difficulty, Level 3, large group

- 39 km in total; trekkers carry their own tents, food, luggage, etc.

- Inca Wonders: five days, moderate physical difficulty, Level 2, small group

- 39 km in total; porters can carry tents, food and equipment if necessary

4 Optional tours are not included in the package. Calculate the extra cost of these. No accommodation is included in optional tours.

5 Confirm the type of package and the total cost of any customized package.

File 6, unit 2, page 23

STUDENT A

You are Bruno Rossi. Look at his profile again in Exercise 2 on page 23 and read the information below.

1 You are a candidate for the job of Assistant Cruise Director. Prepare for your interview. Think of some questions to ask the interviewer.

Bruno Rossi

a Languages: Italian, English and some Spanish. You are studying French at the moment and want to learn Chinese as it's an important new market for Mediterranean cruises.

b You like working with people and meeting and helping guests of so many nationalities. You interact well with people from different cultures.

c You dislike the food on the cruise ship. It's terrible. If you become Assistant Cruise Director, you will sometimes eat with the guests.

d Your ideas for guest activities and entertainment: more live shows with dancers, musicians and singers. People prefer that to discos. Do regular guest surveys to find out what people like and don't like about the entertainment.

2 Now you are the interviewer. Prepare to interview the third candidate: Julie Quinn. Look at her profile again in Exercise 3 on page 23 and prepare questions for the interview.

File 7, unit 4, page 37

STUDENT A

You are a tour guide. Plan a one-day tour of your local area. Explain to a representative of UNESCO why you think one of the historic buildings should be a World Heritage site.

- Include five interesting facts about the area. Invent them if necessary.
- Tell an interesting anecdote about the history of a building, or the people who once lived/worked there.
- Explain why you think your chosen building should be a World Heritage site.
- Be prepared to answer any questions during the tour.

When you have finished, swap roles and then inform the class of your decision.

File 8, unit 3, page 29

STUDENT A

1 Phone the Edinburgh TIC to find out about bike hire in the city. You want to hire bicycles for you and your young family for a few hours on Monday or Tuesday. Ask about prices and get the telephone number to make the booking.

2 You work at the Edinburgh TIC. Look at this information and answer Student B's questions.

Our Dynamic Earth

Our Dynamic Earth takes you on a journey through our planet's past, present and future, with interactive exhibits and impressive technology, including a four-dimensional and three-dimensional experience.

Opening Times: 10 a.m. to 5.30 p.m. Wednesday–Sunday (closed Monday and Tuesday)

Last entry: one hour 30 minutes before closing

Tickets

Adult: £11.50

Child (3–15 yrs): £7.50

Under three years: free

Student/Senior: £9.75

10% discount if you purchase online

File 9, unit 9, page 81

STUDENT B

You are a guest at the Hotel Miami. Ask to check out and query these items on your folio that you received this morning.

Name of guest:	Mr Barry Smith
Total of nights:	two nights at US $60 per night
Room type:	standard single room
Pre-paid:	50%
Balance due:	US $60 for one night, plus these items

Room service – one herbal tea, one cheese sandwich (you are vegetarian)

Room fridge – no items taken (you are allergic to nuts and don't drink juice)

Laundry – one shirt

Explain that you have lost your room key (it's probably in the pool). Your room number is 313. You are a frequent business traveller and have enjoyed your stay at the hotel.

File 10, unit 3, page 29

STUDENT B

1 You work at the Edinburgh TIC. Look at the information about bike hire and answer Student A's questions.

Bike Hire in Edinburgh

Shop name: Pedal King
Address: 84 Bridge Street, near Waverley train station
Opening times: six days a week (Tuesday–Sunday 9 a.m. to 5 p.m.)
Telephone: 0145 340 099
Adult and child bikes for hire
Prices: Adult's bike half day £10, full day £15. Children's bike half day £6, full day £8.

2 Phone the Edinburgh TIC to find out about Our Dynamic Earth. Get the opening hours, and ticket prices. You want to go on Monday.

File 11, unit 2, page 23

STUDENT B

You are the interviewer. You are going to interview Bruno Rossi for the job of Assistant Cruise Director.

1 Read Bruno's profile again in Exercise 2 on page 23 and prepare questions for the interview.

2 Now you are Julie Quinn. Look at her profile again in Exercise 3 on page 23 and read the information below.

Julie Quinn

a Languages: You learnt some Japanese as part of your degree. You can speak Spanish.

b You like being part of a team with the other cruise staff – and all the beautiful destinations you can visit for free!

c You dislike it when the weather is very bad because you get seasick but the experienced staff tell you that gets better with time.

d Your ideas for guest activities and entertainment: more activities for children and families. The market is changing and more young families are choosing cruise ship holidays. Also, organize port excursions especially for families, e.g. trips to zoos and theme parks.

File 12, unit 3, page 31

Visitor Survey report

We asked 600 visitors during the months of July and August to complete this card to find out about their level of satisfaction with the service and information provided. The results (in percentages) are given here:

Welcome by staff
Poor 5%   Satisfactory 40%   Good 50%   Excellent 5%

Knowledge of staff
Poor 3%   Satisfactory 22%   Good 60%   Excellent 15%

Speed of service
Poor 0%   Satisfactory 10%   Good 70%   Excellent 20%

Leaflets and information
Poor 20%   Satisfactory 25%   Good 50%   Excellent 5%

Shop and souvenirs on sale
Poor 35%   Satisfactory 40%   Good 25%   Excellent 0%

Displays
Poor 10%   Satisfactory 35%   Good 50%   Excellent 5%

Comments and suggestions for improvement:
The results show that most visitors are happy with the speed of the service but typical comments were 'The assistants were fast and knowledgeable but not very friendly' and 'The assistant didn't say hello, goodbye or smile during the conversation.'
Some visitors were surprised that there were leaflets in English and French but not in other languages, particularly Spanish. The shop received the worst results for satisfaction. Customers said that there is not a good variety of souvenirs and gifts, and most did not buy anything. Visitors also commented that the displays are mainly posters that are not very interesting or interactive for children. They want more multimedia displays.

File 13, unit 4, page 33

You are tour guides offering a two-hour tour in the area where you live or work/study. Prepare your tour and include these points.

- Name and type of tour, e.g. walking/bus tour, historic, cultural, gastronomic
- Describe the places of interest. What is the main attraction?
- Do you have specialist knowledge of the area? If so, what?
- Does the tour include transport, a meal or refreshments? If so, what and where?
- Price per person? Discounts?

Now work in groups. Present your tour to the group. Persuade the visitors to go on your tour and be prepared to answer any questions.

When you have finished, vote on the best tour in your group. Why was it the most interesting?

File 14, unit 1, page 15

STUDENT B

You are Mark. You would like to book a two-week package in Peru. Your budget is now US $4,500 for two people. You would like to do and see as much as possible. The travel consultant phones you to confirm the booking. Ask about these details and take notes so that you can check the total cost at the end.

1 Confirm your travel dates: 16–30 August.

2 Ask if flights (from Mexico City), accommodation, transfers, guides, entrance tickets, tours and all meals are included in the package.

3 Check details about the Inca Trail tour. How long is it? You and your sister are experienced at walking and you'd prefer to go with a smaller group, and without a guide.

4 You prefer to do sand-boarding for two days with one night in Huacachina. (Four hours is a long trip from Lima.) Ask if this is possible.

5 Check the total cost of the package.

File 15, unit 4, page 37

STUDENT B

You are a representative of UNESCO. You are on a tour of your region for buildings that could become World Heritage sites. Think of some possible historic buildings.
• Listen to a tour guide's information about the area.
• Make a note of any interesting facts or anecdotes about the place.
• Think of five or six questions to ask during the tour.
• Decide if you think it should be a World Heritage site.
When you have finished, swap roles and then inform the class of your decision.

File 16, unit 5, page 41

STUDENT B

Roleplay the check-in situations with Student A. Use the check-in stages 1–7 in Exercise 2 on page 40.

Student B: check-in 1
• You are a guest checking into the Petrovskaya Hotel.
• Your name is Otabek Karimov.
• You reserved a single room for three nights.
• You have a heavy suitcase and need a porter to help you.

Student B: check-in 2
• You are a receptionist at the Victoria Hotel.
• Confirm that the guest's reservation is a junior suite for seven nights.
• Breakfast is not included in the reservation.
• Try to sell the guest the hotel's buffet dinner. There is a 15% discount on the buffet dinner this week.
• The guest's room is on the fourteenth floor.

File 17, unit 5, page 45

STUDENT A

Situation 1

You are a receptionist at a five-star hotel. Some guest rooms need renovating. It is the hotel's policy to offer these rooms at 75% discount until the renovation work begins. Listen to the guest and try to deal with their complaint.

Situation 2

You are returning from your holiday abroad. Your flight arrives at 11 p.m. You have a reservation for tonight at a hotel near the airport because you don't want to drive 200 km to your home tonight. Your flight is diverted to another airport because of a storm and you don't arrive at your hotel until 4 a.m. You could not ring the hotel about your late arrival because you were on the plane. You decide to complain to reception.

File 18, unit 6, page 53

You manage a fast food restaurant together. Decide what type of fast food restaurant it is. Write a short menu for your restaurant. Then change partners. Show your new partner your menu and roleplay taking an order.

1 Greet the customer.

2 Show the customer your menu.

3 Ask the customer if she/he wants to eat in or take away.

4 Take the customer's order.

5 Ask if your customer wants extra items, e.g. extra fillings, salads, drinks, cakes.

6 Tell your customer the cost and give the customer her/his change.

Swap roles and roleplay being the customer.

File 19, unit 6, page 55

STUDENT A

You are the Event Manager at the Bella Centre, a large hotel and conference centre. Phone the Catering Manager about the catering for an event. The details are:

- Client's name: Norton Travel Company
- Date of the event: 13 February
- Venue: the Picasso rooms
- Number of guests: approx. 650 (to be confirmed)
- Type of event: sit down
- Time of day: lunchtime
- Formal or informal: formal
- Choice of serving pieces: plates, glassware and silver cutlery
- Special requests: vegetarian meals (numbers to be confirmed)
- Price per head?

File 20, unit 6, page 58

STUDENT B

Exchange information with Student A to complete Katrina's sales data.

e.g. What's the menu price of the Australian fillet steak?

*Menu item	Cost	Menu price	Sold per week
Australian fillet steak	$9.50	1 ___	100
T-bone steak	2 ___	$24	60
Lamb ribs	$10	$28.50	3 ___
Grilled chicken breast	$6	$23	4 ___
Katrina's beef burger	$5	5 ___	100
Veggie burger (contains nuts)	6 ___	$20.50	15

All main courses are served with chips or baked potatoes. Other vegetables can be ordered as side dishes.

File 21, unit 7, page 63

STUDENT B

Ask and answer questions to complete the missing information.

- The Sahara Desert is the largest hot desert in the world. It covers 11 countries and there are sand dunes as high as 180 m.
- The Red Sea Reef off the coasts of Egypt, Sudan and Eritrea is 1,995 km long. There are more than 1,100 species of fish here.
- Mount Kilimanjaro in northern Tanzania is the highest mountain in Africa at 5,895 m. The second highest mountain, Mount Kenya, has three peaks over [6]___ m.
- The Serengeti plains are located in north Tanzania and southwest Kenya. Some [7]___ larger mammal species, including wildebeest, zebras and buffalo, and about [8]___ bird species are found here.
- Aldabra Atoll, a coral island in the shape of a ring in the Indian Ocean, is [9]___ km long and [10]___ km wide.

File 22, unit 8, page 68

STUDENT A

Ask and answer questions about London Heathrow airport to complete the table.

1	number of airlines operating at Heathrow	[1]___
2	number of destinations Heathrow serves	183 destinations in 90 countries
3	number of passengers arriving and departing	on average [3]___ per day
4	busiest terminal (passenger numbers)	Terminal 5 with 26.3 million passengers per year
5	number of international passengers	[5]___ million per year
6	total employment at Heathrow Airport	76,500 people

File 23, unit 8, page 73

STUDENT B

1 You are a passenger at the check-in desk. Your suitcase is heavy because you bought a lot of clothes and souvenirs on holiday, and you spent all your money. Now you're going home happy at the end of a great holiday.

2 You are a flight attendant. The flight today is very full and it was delayed by two hours, so passengers are more demanding than usual. There were no special meals ordered for passengers in your section of the cabin.

File 24, unit 9, page 77

STUDENT A

You are the EHK. Ask the new housekeeper about what he/she has or hasn't done. Use the ideas in the box and some of your own. When you have finished, swap roles and repeat the task.

e.g. *A: Have you aired the pillows in the presidential suite yet?*

> air the pillows
> count the blankets in the wardrobes
> have a coffee break   mop the floors
> put out clean towels   remove any carpet stains
> take the dirty linen to the laundry

File 25, unit 5, page 45

STUDENT B

Situation 1

You found a bargain offer on the internet for a weekend in a famous five-star hotel at 75% discount and booked it as an anniversary treat for your husband/wife. Unfortunately, when you get there you find the room is small, dark and shabby. The view from the window is a car park and there are tiles missing from the bathroom wall. The breakfast buffet is not very appetizing. You decide to complain to reception.

Situation 2

You are the receptionist in a hotel near the airport. It is 4 a.m. It is your hotel's policy to cancel any room bookings if guests do not ring before midnight to say that they will be late. It is clearly stated on your website and on the confirmation, and guests do not receive refunds in these circumstances. Any guests who arrive late can pay for another room at the walk-in rate, which is more expensive than booking in advance. Listen to the guest and try to deal with their complaint.

File 26, unit 9, page 79

STUDENT A

1 Ask Student B questions to complete the information about the Pera Palace Hotel.

e.g. *When did the Pera Palace Hotel first open?*

Pera Palace Hotel, Istanbul

Turkey's first Western hotel opened in [1]_____. Designed in both Western and [2]_____ styles, its refurbished suites today have antique furniture and modern fittings including [3]_____. Restoration took [4]_____ years and cost [5]_____ (US $32.5 m). The hotel has elegant themed suites, such as the Agatha Christie suite and the Atatürk Museum Room. Celebrity guests include Kemal Atatürk, Ernest Hemingway, [6]_____, Alfred Hitchcock and [7]_____, who wrote *Murder on the Orient Express* in [8]_____ in 1934. Today you can still board the Venice Simplon [9]_____ at Sirkeci station for the Istanbul–Venice journey. This is made only once a year.

2 Read this information about the Peace Hotel and answer Student B's questions.

Peace Hotel, Shanghai

Opened: 1929 as the Cathay Hotel
Former owner: Victor Sassoon, lived on the 10th floor
Style: guestrooms have Art Deco furniture with modern fittings, e.g. plasma stereo TV, a bath-side LCD screen, Blu-Ray DVD player, Wi-Fi and espresso machine
Additions: a presidential suite on the 10th floor, a new extension with an indoor pool and spa
Restoration: three years (cost unknown)
Celebrity guests: Charlie Chaplin, Noël Coward, who wrote *Private Lives* while staying at the hotel, Ernest Hemingway, Muhammad Ali and Bill Clinton
Special interest: the famous 'Nine Nations Suites'; eight restaurants

File 27, unit 8, page 68

STUDENT B

Ask and answer questions about London Heathrow airport to complete the table.

1	number of airlines operating at Heathrow	86
2	number of destinations Heathrow serves	2___ destinations in 90 countries
3	number of passengers arriving and departing	on average 190,100 per day
4	busiest terminal (passenger numbers)	Terminal 5 with 4___ million passengers per year
5	number of international passengers	64.7 million
6	total employment at Heathrow Airport	6___ people

File 28, unit 9, page 81

STUDENT A

You work on front desk at the Hotel Miami. Look at the information for a guest's folio. Deal with the guest's queries, address any complaints and correct any errors. Offer the guest a special promotion if they make an advanced booking at check-out.

Name of guest: B. Smith
Room number: 413
Total of nights: four nights at US $100.00 per night
Room type: an executive suite
Pre-paid: 25%
Balance due: US $100.00 plus these items
Room fridge – one packet of nuts, one chocolate bar
Laundry – one dress (dry-cleaned)
Room service – one bottle of orange juice, two chicken curry
You have receipts signed by Brenda Smith. There is a $10.00 charge for lost room keys. Hair and beauty treatment is charged separately.

File 29, unit 9, page 83

STUDENT A

You are Tracy from Cleaning on Wheels. Look at your information and prepare what you will say.

- The hotel has many windows.
- Some areas have stainless steel surfaces that are difficult to clean but you know of a good solution – it's a secret recipe of your grandmother's!
- There are paint marks on furniture and carpets but you use a very effective acid solvent.
- Two of your workers are sick. If the hotel wants two teams, you need to find two employees at short notice.
- Your firm usually only works in New Hampshire. Say you have worked at the hotel as an HK before and that you will supervise the cleaning.
- Your estimated cost is $2,220 ($384 x five, eight-hour shifts + $300 for cleaning materials). You think the clean-up will take three days.

File 30, unit 10, page 89

STUDENT A

1 You are a holiday rep. You have been offered a job at a resort in Antalya on the Mediterranean coast of Turkey. You don't have any experience. Ask your new boss about the salary. Your friends tell you the average pay is 1,100–1,400 TRY per month but there are possible benefits, such as free accommodation, uniforms, flights home, food allowance and good working hours. Try to negotiate the best possible salary and benefits package.

2 You are a travel agent in the UK. You want to negotiate the price of a group of 12 (six business travellers with their partners) for five days in a health and wellness spa in Göl Türkbükü. Your first preference is the first week of August but another week between June and September will be acceptable if you can negotiate a good deal. The spa is on the Bodrum peninsular in Turkey. Phone the spa's manager. The manager has given you good discounts on corporate packages before. Your budget is €12,500 – same as last year. Persuade the manager to give you a discount.

File 31, unit 9, page 79

STUDENT B

1 Read this information about the Pera Palace Hotel and answer Student A's questions.

Pera Palace Hotel, Istanbul

Opened:	1892
Style:	Western (neo-classical and Art Nouveau) and Oriental
Suites:	antique furniture and modern fittings, e.g. electronic window blinds
Additions:	themed suites, e.g. the Agatha Christie suite and the Atatürk Museum Room painted in pink
Restoration:	four years; cost £20 million (US $32.5 m)
Celebrity guests:	Kemal Atatürk, Ernest Hemingway, Greta Garbo, Alfred Hitchcock and Agatha Christie, who wrote her famous novel in room 411
Special interest:	board the Venice Simplon Orient Express at Sirkeci station for the Istanbul–Venice journey (only goes once a year)

2 Ask Student A questions to complete the information about the Peace Hotel.

e.g. *When did the Peace Hotel first open?*

Peace Hotel, Shanghai

China's most famous hotel opened in ¹_____ as the Cathay Hotel. Its former owner was Sir Victor Sassoon who lived on the ²_____ floor. The refurbished guestrooms have Art Deco furniture with modern fittings, e.g. plasma stereo TV, a bath-side LCD screen, Blu-Ray ³_____ and ⁴_____. There is now a presidential suite on the 10th floor and a new indoor ⁵_____. Restoration took ⁶_____ years. Famous guests include ⁷_____, Noël Coward, who wrote *Private Lives* while staying at the hotel, Ernest Hemingway, Muhammad Ali and ⁸_____. The famous 'Nine Nations Suites' have been redesigned and there are a total of ⁹_____ restaurants to choose from.

File 32, unit 10, page 91

STUDENT B

Read the information below. Take turns with Student A to ask to ask and answer questions to find out more information about Isan.

Tourism in Thailand

The weather: in the rainy season in Thailand the weather is cooler, accommodation is cheaper and there are fewer tourists. It's also an excellent time for river rafting. Isan is the least developed region of Thailand, although it has the best value hotels.

Isan region

Isan is the least visited region in Thailand but it has a rich cultural heritage, influenced by the Lao and Khmer cultures. The Khmers ruled here from the 9th to 14th centuries. There are Khmer temple ruins near Phimai and Buri ram.

Prasat Hin Phimai: This historical site in Phimai town is an important Buddhist temple complex, which was originally from the Khmer period. The temple is built of sandstone and has been beautifully restored.

Surin: Surin is famous for its silk, its elephants and its first ruler, Phraya Surin. Surin's big attraction is the Elephant Round-up every November. Between 150 and 200 elephants are led into Surin by their mahouts (riders). There are shows and spectators can take rides.

Phnom Rung: This temple, situated at the top of an extinct volcano in Buri ram, is a fine example of Khmer architecture. You can see the rising sun through all 15 doors on the western side at Songkran, when Thais celebrate their New Year in April.

File 33, unit 4, page 39

STUDENT B

RockHeavyFest

Get ready for *the* rock and heavy metal festival, near Vienna. Rock bands and goth fans from all over Europe: Austria, Germany, Sweden, Poland, the Czech Republic, Croatia, Portugal, Spain and Italy, etc.
Click here for line-up and videos.
Bring a tent. Bring your friends. Bring your bike and leathers. We will rock you!
Prices (ticket only): €65 (one day), €150 (three days), €250 (five days)
Basic RHFest package: two tickets, five days + camping (for two-person tent plus car), €720 for two
Deluxe RHFest package: two tickets, five days + hostel for two (big rock breakfast incl.) near festival ground, €850.

File 34, unit 9, page 83

STUDENT B

You are Dean from Clean & Sheen. Look at your information and prepare what you will say.

- You use the latest pressure washing method for cleaning windows.

- You use environmentally-safe products for stainless steel surfaces.

- There are paint marks on furniture and carpets but you use good quality solvents that are safe.

- At Clean & Sheen you have regular breaks – a ten-minute break every two hours.

- You have been responsible for operations like this one in other hotels in all six of New England's states – you can offer to email some testimonials.

- Your estimated cost is $3,050 ($500 x five, eight-hour shifts + $550 for materials). You think the clean-up will take at least five days.

File 35, unit 10, page 89

STUDENT B

1 You are the manager of a resort in Antalya on the Mediterranean coast of Turkey. You offer a job to a new sales rep who has no experience. Be prepared to answer questions about the salary. You offer 1,100 TRY per month but you also provide free accommodation, free uniforms, one free flight home per year and a food allowance. Sales reps work six days a week and the working hours are usually about 12 hours a day.

2 You are the manager of a health and wellness spa in the charming town of Göl Türkbükü on the Bodrum peninsular in Turkey. A British travel agent phones you about a corporate group booking. The agent has sent clients to your spa before. The spa is full in July and August but you can offer dates in June and September. The spa in Göl Türkbükü is very popular, so prices have gone up ten percent this year. Your hotel chain has a sister wellness centre in Central Anatolia that isn't on the coast but is more economic (ten percent cheaper than Göl Türkbükü) and there are still rooms available in August. Persuade the agent to book the spa in Anatolia.

File 36, unit 9, page 77

STUDENT B

You are a new housekeeper. Answer the EHK's questions about what you have/haven't done. Use the ideas in the box and your own ideas for things that you have done. When you have finished, swap roles and repeat the task.

> e.g. *B: No, I haven't. But I've cleaned the bathrooms on the fifth floor.*

air the rooms   change the sheets
clean the bathrooms
count the chairs on the balconies
do the rooms on the sixth floor
replace the toiletries
take out the rubbish

File 37, unit 9, page 81

STUDENT B

You are a guest at the Hotel Miami. Ask to check out and query these items on your folio that you received this morning.

Name of guest: Mrs Brenda Smith
Room number: 413
Total of nights: four nights at US $100.00 per night
Room type: an executive suite
Pre-paid: 25%
Balance due: US $100.00 plus these items
Room fridge – one packet of nuts (no chocolate – you're on a diet)
Laundry – one dress (dry-cleaned)
Hair and beauty salon – one wash and style, one manicure
Room service – one bottle of orange juice, two chicken curry
You have receipts for the laundry service and hairdresser's. You and your husband are frequent travellers and have enjoyed your stay at the hotel (it was your wedding anniversary).

File 38, unit 1, page 13

STUDENT B

Booking 1

You are Charlie Sierra from a local travel agency. You want to book a table for 15 people at a hotel restaurant in Ottawa, Canada.

- The hotel has various thematic restaurants – you prefer the Indian restaurant because it has private rooms.

- Phone and make a reservation for 9.00 p.m. for the first Saturday of next month.

- Be prepared to spell your name and give your phone number.

Booking 2

You work as a booking agent for *Melbourne Entertainment*. Take a phone booking for the Australian Open.

- Offer the caller a promotional offer – one free ticket for every eight seats.

- Tickets are priced at A$25.00, A$39.00 or A$50.00 and the booking fee is included.

- Remember to ask for the caller's full name, as it appears on the credit card, the credit card number, a phone number and an email address.

File 39, unit 6, page 55

STUDENT B

You are the Catering Manager at the Bella Centre, a large hotel and conference centre. The Event Manager at the hotel phones you about the catering for an event. The information you need is:

- client's name
- date of the event
- venue
- number of guests
- type of event
- time of day
- formal or informal
- choice of serving pieces (disposable or glass and china)

Offer to email the Event Manager some options for the menu with the price per head.

GRAMMAR REFERENCE

Present simple question forms

1 *Be*

To make questions with the verb *be*, we put the verb before the subject or subject pronoun.

*Tina **is** our guide.* → ***Is** Tina our guide?*

*They **are** Chinese tourists.* → ***Are** they Chinese tourists?*

2 Other main verbs

Put the auxiliary verb *do/does* before the subject to make questions.

The main verb is in the infinitive form without *to*.

The word order is: *do/does* + subject + infinitive.

You work in a hotel. → ***Do** you **work** in a hotel?*

He speaks French. → ***Does** he **speak** French?*

She likes her job. → ***Does** she **like** her job?*

They go to Paris every year. → ***Do** they **go** to Paris every year?*

3 Questions words

Put question words, e.g. *who, what, when, how, where, why* at the start of a question before *be*.

Where are you from?

What time is it?

Put question words before the auxiliary verb *do/does* in a question with a main verb.

The word order is: questions word(s) + *do/does* + subject + infinitive.

How do you spell your surname?

How much does the tour cost?

When do the group arrive?

Present simple and present continuous

PRESENT SIMPLE

1 Use

We use the present simple to talk about things that are always or usually true.

*We **specialize** in city tours.*

*Barry **has** a cooking diploma.*

We also use the present simple to describe routines, habits, actions or situations that happen all the time.

*They always **clean** the rooms in the mornings.*

2 Form

The third person singular ends with *-s*, e.g. *clean* → *clean**s**, go → go**es**, have → ha**s***.

*He need**s** to make sure his assistant know**s** what she ha**s** to do.*

We use *don't* (*do not*) or *doesn't* (*does not*) to make the negative form.

*We **don't** usually **organize** tours.*

*I'm **not**/He **isn't** a general manager.*

To make questions, use *do* or *does*.

The word order is: question word(s) + *do/does* + subject + infinitive

*Does he **have** a diploma?*

*Where **do** you **work**?*

In questions with the verb *be* change the word order.

***Are** you responsible for accommodation?*

***Is** he the manager?*

For short answers, use the appropriate form of *do* only.

***Do** you **use** a computer booking system? Yes, we **do**./No, we **don't**.*

***Does** she **like** her job? Yes, she **does**./No, she **doesn't**.*

3 Adverbs of frequency

Use these adverbs before the main verb but after the verb *be*.

*I **usually talk** to the events manager.*

*Does he **often work** at weekends?*

*She **is often** busy at this time.*

PRESENT CONTINUOUS

1 Use

We use the present continuous to describe activities that are happening now.

*Jane **is talking** to the travel agent at the moment.*

*She **isn't booking** online.*

We also use the present continuous to describe temporary activities, often with time expressions, e.g. *at the moment/now, this week/month/year*.

*We **are studying** English for tourism this year.*

*He **isn't working** at the moment.*

2 Non-action (stative) verbs

Have is usually a non-action verb like *be, like* and *want*. But some expressions with *have* can have a continuous form, e.g. *have breakfast/lunch/dinner/a coffee/a meal/a shower/a bath/a good time*.

*They're **serving** breakfast at the moment.*

*She's **having** a coffee break.*

For more information on stative verbs see page 117.

See Unit 7 for information about the use of the present continuous in the future.

3 Form

For the positive form, use the correct form of *be* + verb in the *-ing* form.

*I'm help**ing** new staff this week.*

*The chef **is planning** today's menu.*

The negative form is with the negative form of *be*.

*I**'m not** recruiting new staff this month.*

*She **isn't** dealing with a guest right now.*

The word order is: question word(s) + *be* + *-ing* form.

***Are** you living in student accommodation?*

***Is** she inspecting the rooms now?*

*What **are** they doing at the moment?*

For short answers, use the appropriate form of *be* only.

***Are** you staying in a lodge this week? Yes, I **am**./ No, I**'m not**.*

***Is** he training new staff? Yes, he **is**./No, he **isn't**./ No, he**'s not**.*

Comparative and superlative forms

1 Form

The table below shows the comparative and superlative forms for adjectives of one syllable and for two-syllable adjectives ending in *y*.

high cheap safe	higher (than) cheaper (than) safer (than)	the highest the cheapest the safest	Use **-er** and **-est** for most one-syllable adjectives.
large	larger (than)	the largest	Use **-r** and **-st** for one-syllable adjectives that end with *e*.
big	bigger (than)	the biggest	Double the final consonant for one-syllable adjectives ending with a vowel and a consonant.
happy early	happier (than) earlier (than)	the happiest the earliest	Add **-ier** and **-iest** for two-syllables adjectives that end with *y*.

We use *more* and *the most* to make comparative and superlative forms for:

Adjectives with two or more syllables.

*modern → **more** modern, **the most** modern*

*comfortable → **more** comfortable, **the most** comfortable*

Adjectives with one syllable that end in *-ed*.

*organized → **more** organized, **the most** organized*

2 We use *much* or *far* to modify a comparative adjective.

*New York is **much** bigger than London.*

*This suite is **far more** comfortable than the standard room.*

3 Use *(not) as* adjective *as* in comparisons of equality.

*Is Amsterdam **as** big **as** London?*

*The hotel wasn't **as** good **as** we expected.*

4 Irregular forms

good → better → the best

bad → worse → the worst

far → further → the furthest

Past simple

USE

1 We use the past simple to talk about finished actions at a definite time in the past.

*Mozart **came** from Salzburg. He **died** in 1791.*

*They **didn't return** to the hotel until 9 p.m.*

*When **did** the coach **leave**?*

The past simple is often used with these time expressions:

He arrived last night/Tuesday/week/month/year.

*We **didn't have** many visitors six hours/months/ years ago.*

***Did** she **die** on (date) in (year)?*

***Did** you **enjoy** the tour yesterday/this morning?*

*When **did** visitors **start** coming here?*

2 Form

Add *-ed* to regular verbs to form the past.

*They book**ed** a table for eight.*

*Henry VIII play**ed** tennis at Hampton Court.*

Some verbs are irregular. See page 117 for a list of irregular verbs.

*They **went** on a London black cab tour.*

*The Romans **built** London's first bridge.*

Use *didn't* + the infinitive form of the verb.

*We **didn't have** time to see everything.*

*She **didn't send** the e-brochures yesterday.*

Use question word(s) + *did* + subject + the infinitive form of the verb.

*When **did** you **book** the tour?*

*What **did** he **say**?*

*What time **did** they **arrive**?*

For short answers, use the appropriate form of *did* only.

Did you **book** *a tour yesterday? Yes, I* **did**.*/No, I* **didn't**.

Did she **book** *a tour yesterday? Yes, she* **did**.*/No she* **didn't**.

4 Past simple passive

We use the past passive for describing processes, when we don't know who did something, or when we are more interested in what happened and not who did it.

The hotel **was renovated** *in 2010.*

The Tower of London **was built** *over 900 years ago.*

When we know who was responsible for the action, we use *by.*

The Houses of Parliament buildings were **designed by** *Sir Charles Barry.*

Form the past passive with *was/were* + the past participle.

The hotel **wasn't refurbished** *until 2010.*

Was *the table* **reserved**?

Modal verbs

OFFERS

1 Use the modal auxiliary verbs *can, may* and *shall* in questions to offer to do things for other people.

2 Put the modal verb before the subject or subject pronoun to form a question. The main verb is in the infinitive form without *to.*

Can/May/Shall *I help you with your luggage?*

May sounds more formal than *can* and *shall.*

3 We also use *I will* but not *I shall* to offer to do something.

I'll call *the porter for you.*

We can use *would + you + like …?* to make polite offers.

Would you like *to see the dessert menu?*

Would you like *help with your luggage?*

REQUESTS

1 We use the modal auxiliary verbs *can* and *could* in questions to ask other people to do things.

2 Put the modal verb before the subject or subject pronoun to form a question. The main verb is in the infinitive form without *to.*

Can/Could *you repeat that, please?*

Could is more indirect and sounds more polite than *can* when making requests.

3 It is also possible to use *May + I …?* to make formal requests.

May *I have your passport, please?*

Countable and uncountable nouns

1 Form

Countable nouns have a singular and plural form. You can count them.

Use *a/an* before a singular countable noun.

a table, *an* omelette, *a* knife, *a* guest, *a* review, *a* serviette

Uncountable nouns do not have a plural form. You cannot count them, e.g. *water, milk, salt, rice, coffee, sugar.*

Many nouns can be countable and uncountable.

She ordered **some** *chicken for lunch. (some = a portion of the bird)*

She ordered **a** *chicken for lunch. (a = the whole bird)*

Drinks are usually uncountable. But they can be countable if it's in a cup, glass or other container.

We'd like **two teas** *and* **a coffee**.

An orange juice *and* **a tonic water**, *please.*

2 *Some* and *any*

We use *some* in positive sentences with plural countable nouns and uncountable nouns.

They prepared **some sandwiches** *for lunch.*

There is **some coffee** *in the pot.*

We also use *some* in offers and requests and in questions when we expect the answer to be 'Yes'.

Would you like **some** *more water?*

Can I have **some** *bread?*

In negative sentences and questions with plural countable nouns and uncountable nouns, we use *any.*

She **never** *eats* **any** *vegetables.*

Is there **any** *meat in this dish?*

3 *Much* and *many*

We use *much* in negative sentences and questions with uncountable nouns, e.g. *water, time.*

How **much water** *do you drink?*

We don't have **much time** *for lunch.*

Use *many* in negative sentences and questions with plural countable nouns, e.g. *people, dishes.*

How **many people** *are in the restaurant?*

They don't have **many** *vegetarian* **dishes**.

In formal written texts *much/many* are also common in positive sentences.

Many *guests like to watch the chefs at the action stations.*

4 *a lot of/lots of*

We use *a lot of* or *lots of* with both plural countable nouns and plural uncountable nouns.

There are **a lot of** *customers today.*

There isn't **a lot of** *variety on this menu.*

Is there **lots of** *garlic in this dish?*

Future forms

PRESENT CONTINUOUS

We use the present continuous from to talk about future plans and arrangements.

We're driving to the coast this weekend.

She isn't taking the tour group next week.

Are the guests arriving tonight?

See Unit 2 for information about the present continuous form.

GOING TO + VERB

1 Use

We use going to for future plans, personal intentions and arrangements.

There is not a lot of difference between the present continuous and going to when used to talk about future plans and arrangements.

We also use going to for predictions with present evidence.

The plane's delayed. We're going to be late.

It's going to rain this afternoon. I heard it on the radio.

2 Form

Use be going to + verb

I'm going to fly to Costa Rica this summer.

To make the negative, we use the negative form of the verb be.

They aren't going to stay in the nature lodge tomorrow.

For questions, put the verb be before the subject.

Are you going to visit San José next month?

WILL

1 Use

We use will/won't for predictions about facts and events expected to be true in the future.

We also use will to make spontaneous offers and decisions.

He'll help you with your luggage.

We'll phone a taxi for you.

I'm tired. I think I'll have a siesta.

2 Form

Use will with a main verb for the positive form and won't (will not) with a main verb for the positive form.

We think the new tour will be very popular.

Local people probably won't want a new airport on the island.

To make questions, put will before the subject.

Will we see a lot of crocodiles in the river?

PRESENT SIMPLE

We use the present simple for timetables, programmes and schedules.

The flight leaves at 6 a.m.

We often use the present simple after future time expressions, e.g. after, before, until, as soon as, when, if.

We're going to swim in the river when we finish our walk.

Modal verbs

OBLIGATION

1 We use must and have to in British English when something is a legal obligation or absolutely necessary. In American English, have to is the normal form.

We use must and have to with a main verb.

Passengers must switch off their mobile phones during the flight.

You have to pass a language test to get a pilot's licence.

2 For questions, we usually use have to (not must). To form questions, put the auxiliary verb do/does before the subject.

Do you have to work at the weekend?

Does he have to speak English in his job?

Do I have to go?

3 British English sometimes makes this distinction between must and have to:

Use must mostly to talk about the feelings and wishes of the speaker.

I must study for the tourism exams next week. (I want to do this.)

Use have to mostly to talk about obligations that are 'external', e.g. laws, regulations, agreements, other people's orders.

We have to do three exams next week. (It is university regulations.)

PROHIBITION

We use mustn't, can't and not be allowed to when something is not permitted or is prohibited.

We use mustn't, can't and not be allowed to with a main verb.

You mustn't smoke anywhere inside the airport terminal.

He can't travel without a valid passport.

Passengers are not allowed to use the toilet during take-off and landing.

PERMISSION

We use can and be allowed to when something is permitted.

Use can and be allowed to with a main verb.

You can use electronic devices during the flight.

Clients are allowed to sit in this area.

To form questions with can, put the modal verb before the subject.

Can we sit in here?

To form questions with *be allowed to*, put the verb *be* before the subject.

Are we allowed to sit in here?

ADVICE

Use *should* and *shouldn't* to give advice, and to make suggestions and recommendations.

Use *should* and *shouldn't* with a main verb.

Guests **should** phone the hotel to ask for a late checkout.

Tourists **shouldn't** carry a lot of cash.

Put *should* before the subject to form questions.

Should we translate the instructions into Spanish?

NO OBLIGATION

Use *don't/doesn't have to* when something is not necessary.

Use *don't/doesn't have to* with a main verb.

Personnel with ICAO Level Six **don't have to** do another language test.

She **doesn't have to** wear a uniform in her job.

Present perfect

1 Use

We usually use the present perfect to describe:

An event that hasn't happened yet

She **hasn't cleaned** all the rooms yet. (She's going to clean them in the near future.)

Have you **met** the EHK yet?

Recent events

I**'ve** already **checked** their passports.

The plane **has** just **taken off**.

Life experience

We **have worked** as tour guides before. (at some time in our lives)

Have you ever **been** to Mexico? (at some time in your life)

I**'ve** never **been** to Brazil.

2 *For/since*

We use the time expressions *for* or *since* with the present perfect to describe an event that started in the past and is still continuing in the present.

Use *for* with periods of time.

I have lived in Barcelona **for 20 years/for a long time**. (I still live in Barcelona.)

Use *since* for points in time when something began.

He has worked as a tour guide **since 2010/since he left college**. (He's working as a tour guide now.)

3 Form

The present perfect is formed with *have/has* + past participle.

(See page 117 for a list of irregular verbs.)

Use the contracted forms of *have/has* when speaking.

I**'ve** just **started** a new job.

He**'s** never **worked** on a cruise ship before.

She **hasn't seen** him for two weeks.

Short answers

Have you ever **worked** as an EHK? Yes, I **have**./No, I **haven't**.

Has she ever **flown** before? Yes, she **has**./No, she **hasn't**.

Zero and first conditional

1 Use

We use the zero conditional for things that are always true.

If a hotel **doesn't sell** rooms, it **loses** money.

We **offer** a discount if it**'s** a group booking.

It is possible to substitute *if* for *when*.

When a hotel **doesn't sell** rooms, it **loses** money.

We **offer** a discount **when** it**'s** a group booking.

We use the first conditional for describing real possibilities in the present or future.

If you **give** good service, you **will get** tips from customers. (It is very probable.)

2 Form

If + present + present (zero conditional)

If a guest **uses** room service, she **pays** at checkout.

If + present + will + infinitive (first conditional)

If there **are** online offers, more customers **will book**.

We can change the order of the clauses in conditional sentences.

More customers **will book** if there are online offers.

Use the contracted forms *'ll/won't* when speaking.

They**'ll have** more customers if they lower their prices.

They **won't attract** younger guests if they don't refurbish the hotel.

In short answers, we use the appropriate auxiliary verb.

Does a hotel lose money when it doesn't have full occupancy? Yes, it **does**./No, it **doesn't**.

Will I get a commission if I take more bookings? Yes, you **will**./No, you **won't**.

Irregular verbs

Verb	Past simple	Past participle
be	was/were	been
become	became	become
begin	began	begun
break	broke	broken
bring	brought	brought
build	built	built
burn	burnt/burned	burnt/burned
buy	bought	bought
catch	caught	caught
choose	chose	chosen
come	came	come
cost	cost	cost
cut	cut	cut
deal	dealt	dealt
do	did	done
drink	drank	drunk
drive	drove	driven
eat	ate	eaten
fall	fell	fallen
feel	felt	felt
find	found	found
fly	flew	flown
forget	forgot	forgotten
get	got	got/gotten
give	gave	given
go	went	gone
grow	grew	grown
have	had	had
hear	heard	heard
hit	hit	hit
hold	held	held
keep	kept	kept
know	knew	known
learn	learnt/learned	learnt/learned
leave	left	left
let	let	let
light	lit	lit
lose	lost	lost
make	made	made
meet	met	met
pay	paid	paid
put	put	put
read (riːd)	read /red/	read /red/
ring	rang	rung
run	ran	run
say	said	said
see	saw	seen
sell	sold	sold
send	sent	sent
show	showed	shown
shut	shut	shut
sink	sank	sunk
sit	sat	sat
sleep	slept	slept
speak	spoke	spoken
spend	spent	spent
spill	spilt/spilled	spilt/spilled
stand	stood	stood
steal	stole	stolen
swim	swam	swum
take	took	taken
teach	taught	taught
tell	told	told
think	thought	thought
understand	understood	understood
wake	woke	woken
win	won	won
write	wrote	written

Non-action (stative) verbs

Some verbs are not generally used in the continuous form. The most common non-action verbs are:

1 Verbs expressing likes and dislikes, e.g. *dislike, hate, like, love, need, prefer, want.*

   We **want/would like/would prefer** a room with a sea view.

2 Verbs expressing opinions and beliefs, e.g. *believe, doubt, feel, imagine, know, recognize, see, suppose, think, understand.*

   I **think/imagine/believe** South Korea would be a great place to visit.

3 Verbs expressing the properties something or someone has, e.g. *be, appear, consist of, contain, cost, have, include, lack, look, measure, resemble, seem, smell, sound, taste, weigh.*

   This fish **tastes** strange but it **smells** fine.

   This package **includes** flights and accommodation.

4 Verbs related to possession, e.g. *belong to, have, own, need.*

   This spa **belongs to** a chain.

   I**'ve had** this job for two years.

AUDIO SCRIPT

Unit 1

1.1

1 one, two, three, four, five, six, seven, eight, nine, ten, eleven, twelve, thirteen, fourteen, fifteen, sixteen, seventeen, eighteen, nineteen, twenty

2 twenty-one, thirty-two, forty-three, fifty-four, sixty-five, seventy-six, eighty-seven, ninety-eight

3 a hundred and nine, two hundred and ten, three hundred and eleven, four hundred and twelve, five hundred and thirteen, six hundred and twenty, seven hundred and thirty, eight hundred and forty, nine hundred and fifty

4 a thousand, one thousand five hundred, ten thousand, ten thousand seven hundred and fifty, a hundred thousand, a million, a billion

1.2

1
A How many people are in the group?
B One person cancelled so there are now thirteen.

2
A How old is he now?
B He was fourteen last month.

3
A How many states are there in the USA?
B I'm not sure. I think it's fifty.

4
A You're in room sixty.
B Sorry, which room?
A Room sixty.

5
A Can you serve table seventeen, please?
B Table seventeen, which one is that?
A By the window.

6
A Do you have the address of the hotel?
B Yes, it's number eighteen Park Street.

7
A How much does a taxi cost to the airport?
B About ninety dollars.

1.3

1 one hundred and fifty percent, one and a half, one point five

2 seventy-five percent, three quarters, nought point seven five

3 fifty percent, a half, nought point five

4 thirty-three point three percent, a third, nought point three three

5 twenty-five percent, a quarter, nought point two five

6 twenty percent, a fifth, nought point two

7 twelve and a half percent, an eighth, nought point one two five

8 ten percent, a tenth, nought point one

1.4

According to the World Tourism Organization (WTO), the top region for international tourism is Europe, with 52 percent, more than half the world's total tourism market. France is the world's top destination, with nearly 77 million international arrivals last year. The USA was second, with nearly 60 million. China was in third position with 56 million, and Spain was fourth with 53 million foreign visitors. Another important statistic is the money inbound visitors spend in a country. This is known as 'tourism receipts'. International tourism receipts were 919 billion US dollars last year – that's 693 billion euros. The USA has the top tourism receipts in the world, with 104 billion US dollars. Spain was in second position and France was third. The WTO also collects information on tourists' spending habits. Tourists from Germany are the top spenders on international tourism. They spent 78 billion euros last year. Things are changing fast in the tourism industry and the WTO expects China to be the top international destination within the next five years. China is also showing the fastest growth in spending on international tourism in recent years.

1.5

1

W = Woman, M = Man
W Luigi's Grill. Can I help you?
M Hi! I'd like to book a table for six for Friday night.
W Table for six, this Friday, November the third?
M Uh-huh.
W What time?
M Eight-thirty.
W So, that's a table for six, at eight-thirty this Friday.

2

Hi! It's Helen here, your tour guide. I'm phoning about the times for the coach tour to Malbork Castle. There has been a change. The coach is leaving Gdańsk on Thursday half an hour later, at a quarter to seven in the morning, not a quarter past six. So that's a quarter to seven this Thursday. OK? If there's a problem, please call me. Bye.

3

G = Gianluca, L = Lena
G Star Travel International. Gianluca speaking.
L Hi! It's Lena here from Star Travel in Hamburg. I'm phoning about a change in one of our hotel bookings. It's for Mallorca this July.
G Do you have the details, Lena?
L Sure. It's for two twin rooms with baths at the Palma Marina Hotel from the 15th to the 21st of July in the name of Ben Hartmann.
G So that's seven nights from the 15th to the 21st of July?
L That's right. They'd like an apartment for four, if possible.
G One moment, Lena. I'll see what I can do.

1.6

1
A Do you have the email address?
B Yes, it's information at Rail Europe dot co dot U-K.

A Sorry, can you repeat that, please?
B Yes, it's information at Rail Europe. That's all one word, all lower case, R-A-I-L-E-U-R-O-P-E dot co, dot U-K.
A Dot co, dot U-K. Thanks.

2
A I've got a gmail address. It's Annabel Weiss, that's all one word and lower case, at gmail dot com.
B Do you spell your first name A-double N-A-B-E-L?
A That's right. And the surname is Weiss, with no capital letter. W-E-I-double S. That's 'S' for sugar.
B So that's Annabel Weiss, all lower case?
A That's right – at gmail dot com.

1.7

Part One
R = Reservations, C = Caller
R London Theatre reservations.
C Hello! I'd like to book thirty-four tickets for the musical, *The Lion King*.
R Sorry, is that forty-four tickets for *The Lion King*?
C No, thirty-four. Three, four.
R What day please?
C The 16th or the 23rd of October. Wednesday afternoon would be good.
R One moment please.

1.8

Part Two
R = Reservations, C = Caller
R The first available date is Wednesday the 16th of October, starting at two-thirty. Tickets are priced at thirty pounds fifty.
C Yes, that's fine.
R OK. Could I have your name for the booking then, please?
C It's Vic – V–I–C McKenzie. M-C – that's with a small C, K-E-N-Z-I-E.
R So that's M-C-K-E-N-Z-I and is that E for Echo?
C Yes, that's right.
R Can I have your credit card details, please?
C Sure. It's a Visa card. Number 4-5-9-3, 7-6-8-8, 9 double 0-2, 5-0-2-1.
R 4-5-9-3, 7-6-8-8. Sorry, did you say double 9-0-2?
C No, that's 9 double 0-2, 5-0-2-1.
R OK. And your email address, please? So that I can send you confirmation.
C It's Victor Mckenzie, at A-C dot U-K.
R Vicmckenzie at A-C dot U-K.
C Actually, its Victor, not Vic – V-I-C-T-O-R, followed by McKenzie, all one word, all lower case, at A-C dot U-K.
R OK. Can I just check the booking before I put the payment through? That's thirty-four seats for the 16th of October at two-thirty at the Lyceum Theatre. Is that right?
C Yes.
R OK. We'll send you an email confirming your booking, Mr McKenzie. Please bring it with you when you collect your tickets from the theatre box office.

1.9

G = Gabi Werner, M = Mark Bradford

G Hello, CSAM Travel, Gabi speaking. How can I help you?

M Hi, I'm phoning about holidays to Peru.

G Are you interested in a package with flights and accommodation?

M: Yes.

G And do you have an idea of what you'd like to do?

M Well, I'm travelling with my sister. We both like trekking so we would like to do the Inca trail. And visit Machu Picchu. And maybe the Amazon.

M I see. I'm sure we can help. But first, can I have your name please?

M It's Mark, Mark Bradford. That's B-R-A-D-F-O-R-D.

G B-R-A-D-F-O-R-D, thank you. So, when are you planning to travel, Mark?

M Around the 16th of August. Can you give me some idea about prices?

G Yes, but can I check – what kind of budget do you have?

M About $2,500.

G Well, for example, we have a one-week package including return flights to Cusco, which includes trekking on the Inca trail and Machu Picchu for $1,050 per person.

M One week isn't much time. We want to get a feel for the local culture.

G Let me see, ten days. There's our Peru special for 1,200 US dollars.

M So that's $2,400 for two. That sounds good. Does it include Lake Titicaca? We really want to go there.

G No, I'm sorry, it doesn't. But you can combine tours.

M OK, great!

G And can I check your travel dates, Mark? Did you say Friday the 16th of August?

M 16th of August, yes.

G Returning on the 25th of August?

M Yes, that's fine.

G Great. And can I have your email address please?

M It's Mark dot Bradford at Leeds dot A-C dot U-K.

G A-C dot U-K. OK, I'll send you the details for a ten-day package, Mark. I'll also send you information about our one-week and two-week tours, so you can compare tours and prices.

M Sure. Thanks.

1.10

G = Gabi Werner, M = Mark Bradford

M Hi!

G Hello, It's Gabi here. I'm phoning about your booking.

M Hello Gabi! Did you get my message? I have another $1,000 for our budget, so we're now thinking of going for two weeks.

G Two weeks? That's great, Mark. I can recommend the Incan Wonders package. It includes five days trekking and a five-day jungle tour.

M Yes, that's one option. But does it include sand-boarding? I'd love to try that!

G No, it doesn't but we can customize your package. If you go sand-boarding in Huacachina, it's only four hours from Lima.

M I see it includes the ancient lines in Nazca.

G Yes, you can see the ancient lines in the desert from a plane. It's wonderful.

M But my sister is interested in the mountain train ride that goes from Huancayo to Lima. I hear it's amazing.

G Yes, it is but it's a long trip. And you can only go at weekends.

M Oh, well we can't decide. What do you recommend, Gabi?

G First, can I check – are you now planning to travel the last two weeks in August?

M Yes, that's correct. But remember, we're very interested in meeting local people and getting to know the culture.

G OK. Let me check the details of a two-week vacation and I'll phone you back.

M Thanks, Gabi.

Unit 2

2.1

1

Well, first of all, you need to have excellent customer service skills because you spend all day talking to customers. Being organized is essential and you also need to be very communicative. You can't be afraid to speak to people, if it's a tour operator, a hotel, an airline or if it's a customer in the shop. You have to speak to everyone on every level. You also need good sales skills to sell holiday and travel products to customers. And, of course, good IT skills are essential to find information and make bookings online.

2

You have to be customer-focused and efficient. And you have to stay calm and be patient when passengers are worried or angry about something. Being a good communicator who can interact well with people from different cultures is essential. You have to be a good team worker, too. Basic first aid and medical skills are important.

3

I think when people pay for a tour, they are really paying for the personality. I call it 'the three E's': somebody who's energetic, enthusiastic and entertaining. You have to have a passion for people and you need to be energetic because your job is about helping people to have fun. On a practical level, good organizational skills and languages help. I love it – every day is different.

2.2

1

In the USA, travel agents on full-time contracts can earn between $24,000 and $38,000 a year before tax. The salary depends on your experience, sales skills and the size and location of the agency. I work in a large travel agency in San Francisco and my annual salary is over $30,000 now, for a 40-hour week working Monday to Friday. The salary is low but I also get travel benefits, such as discounts on holidays and free trips with airlines and cruise companies if I sell a package to a group.

2

The working hours are very flexible. I often work weekends and holidays and I'm away from home for days. I usually fly 70 hours a month and work another 40 hours on the ground. My salary is about $3,200 a month – that's over $38,000 a year. And I can increase my pay by $3,000 to $8,000 a year by doing extra flights. And my family and I get big discounts on flights.

3

When I started working as a tour guide, I earned $8 per hour. Now I have a contract and I make $23,000 annually. The pay is low but I travel to exotic locations for free. The working hours can be long on a tour – sometimes I work 14–15 a day. A big advantage is that all my meals, accommodation and transport are free. And my customers usually give tips. The last tour I worked, I made $250 in tips in just five days!

2.3

1

We're asking for a recognized qualification in hospitality for this position and, as the advertisement says, you need at least two years' relevant experience. It gets really busy in the high season, so we need a person who is well-organized and can stay calm in a crisis. Obviously, you need excellent customer service and people management skills to deal with both customers and staff. Since we have a lot of international customers in the restaurant, we need someone who can speak good English and at least one other European language.

2

You don't have to have any particular qualifications to apply for this position but if you have experience supervising kids and enjoy working with children, then this will be an advantage. As it says in the advert, we need people with language skills who can work well in a team. But above all, it's a job about helping people to have fun, so the really important thing is to be energetic and enthusiastic. Basic first aid and medical skills would be extremely useful.

2.4

1 Why do you want to work for us?
2 What do you know about our company?
3 Are you good at working in a team?
4 What are your strengths and weaknesses?
5 Do you have any management experience?
6 Why do you want to leave your present job?
7 Are you prepared to work long hours?
8 What would you like to do in five years' time?
9 Why should we hire you?
10 When can you start?

2.5

I started working on cruise ships three years ago when I finished my degree in tourism. I only planned to do a six-month contract to get some work experience but I had so much fun I decided to stay. One thing that really surprised me was the variety of jobs available on-board and how many opportunities there are. I love being part of the entertainment staff. You have to work very long hours – sometimes twelve or fifteen hours a day but I'm a very energetic and enthusiastic person and I love working with people of all ages. In my present job, I work mainly with children and teenagers. I organize and supervise various activities for them. You have to be very creative and very calm and patient in this job. I also help with the entertainment and activities for adults. And last night, I hosted the karaoke. Now I'd like a job with more responsibility and career prospects.

2.6
I = Interviewer, A = Angelica Davies
I Tell me Angelica, why do you want this job?
A Because it's a great opportunity to use the skills and experience I already have and to learn more.
I What languages do you speak?
A Well, just English. But I would like to learn another European language. I think it's useful, you know, for the job.
I What do you like about working on a cruise ship? And what do you dislike?
A What I like is you can have a lot of fun working as cruise staff. I don't like living in a small cabin but it's not a big problem.
I What ideas do you have for guest entertainment?
A Well, I think we should get local entertainers to come on-board at each port. You know, musicians and dancers who can do a special show, or invite a chef to do a presentation about local food and dishes. So passengers can learn more about the places they are visiting.
I Yes, I see. Some nice ideas. OK, so why should we offer you this job?
A That's a good question. I think I would be a great assistant cruise director. I'm outgoing, I'm a people-person, I have excellent communication and customer service skills, which are essential for the job. I'm good at talking to guests and promoting excursions and I'll be good at promoting the on-board entertainment as well. I'm not an entertainer myself. I can't sing or dance but I'm supervising staff in my present job, and I think that's more important in this role. But most of all, I enjoy making a cruise holiday fun for guests.

Unit 3

3.1
1
Spain has a highly developed tourist industry that offers a wide variety of services to travellers of all ages and budgets – backpackers on low budgets, experienced travellers on cultural visits to heritage sites, as well as family holidaymakers in beach resorts. There are 'oficinas de turismo', or tourist offices, in all major towns and resorts. And we

give information on accommodation, restaurants and of course places to visit and things to do. We also give out town plans, details about leisure activities and festivals like the carnival here in Tenerife, las Fallas in Valencia, or the Easter parades in Seville or Granada. Larger cites around the world usually have a Spanish National Tourist Office and you can also visit the official website at www.spain. info. I think Spanish people are naturally open and welcoming to visitors, so the best information comes from the locals themselves.

2
On the Chinese mainland, there are still not many official Tourist Information Offices. My advice to visitors to China is that they should be careful of travel companies who say they are 'official' organizations. This is because they are often only private travel agents. If you need information on China, the China National Tourism Administration has branches in most countries in the world. They are also called China National Tourist Offices. Off the mainland, Hong Kong and Macau have their own professional tourism agencies. At the Hong Kong Tourism Board where I work, and at The Macau Government Tourism Office, we offer free information, maps and advice. And you'll find there are Visitor Information Centres in the airports, both in Macau and Hong Kong. Macau has its own Business Tourism Centre, too.

3.2
About five million people visit the Edinburgh region annually, and we get thousands of enquiries each month. We are here to help with information on city attractions, local events and short breaks in other destinations in Scotland. You can also buy gifts and souvenirs here. And we can book a hotel or B&B for you. The most common questions we get are: 'Can I have a map of the city?' and 'What are the local attractions?' Visitors can get a free map here and information about all the city's attractions. You can also buy the Edinburgh Pass here, which is a sightseeing pass that includes discounts on more than 30 attractions, as well as bus tours and city buses. The pass also includes special offers for restaurants, cafés, shops and tours. It's not only tourists visiting the city who come to us. A lot of local people also contact us for information about the holidays and breaks in the rest of Scotland and the UK.

3.3
A = VIC Assistant, C = Caller
A VisitScotland Information Centre. Paula speaking. How can I help you?
C Hello! Is that the Edinburgh tourist office?
A Yes, that's right. Can I help you?
C Yes, we'd like some information about tours.
A Sorry, do you mean the guided tours or the bus tours?
C I don't know. Can you tell me about both?

A Certainly. There are four bus tours. They are hop-on hop-off services.
C I see. Which is the best tour?
A Well, the most popular one is the City Sightseeing Tour. It leaves from Waverley Bridge, outside Waverley train station every 15 minutes. You can get off the bus at any of the stops along the way, visit the sights and then get back on another tour bus.
C When does the service operate?
A It's a 24-hour service so the ticket is valid on all the tour buses all day.
C How long is the tour?
A If you stay on the bus, it's approximately 60 minutes.
C Sounds like a good idea. How much does it cost?
A Adult tickets cost £15, senior citizen and student tickets cost £13 and for children under sixteen tickets are £6.
C And the guided tours?
A There are several guided walking tours. A popular one is the tour of the old town. It starts here from the Tourist Information Centre on Princes Street and lasts about 90 minutes. Tours start at 10 a.m., noon, 2.30 p.m. and 4.30 p.m. every day in summer. The cost is £9 for adults. It's half price for children under eight and senior citizens.
C I think we'll go on the bus tour this afternoon.
A Right. You can buy the tickets from the driver on the bus, or the ticket seller on Waverley Bridge.
C Great! Many thanks for your help.
A You're welcome. Would you like anything else?
C No thanks.
A Thank you for calling the centre. Good bye.

3.4
As part of the study, I telephoned, sent an email enquiry and made a personal visit to the visitor centres. My email asked for a list of places to stay in the area. The first centre replied with the information within 48 hours but the second centre didn't answer me. I sent the email again but still did not get a reply. In the next test, I phoned to ask about things to see and do in the area. I waited more than five rings for both centres to answer the phone. There was no standard practice for answering the telephone in the centres. In one, the assistant gave the name of the centre and her name at the start of the call. This assistant was friendly, polite and knowledgeable. The assistant in the other centre was less professional and told me to consult the website or visit the office in person for information. The second centre also put me on hold for five minutes without explanation, and I abandoned the call. In the third test, I visited the centres in person. The staff welcome in the first centre was excellent – the assistant smiled, made eye contact and was well informed. The assistants in the other centre ignored me when I went in. When I asked for information, they gave me leaflets. The first centre was clean, well decorated and organized. But there was a lot of paper and boxes on the floor in the second one I

visited, and the paint on the walls was old and dirty.

Unit 4

4.1

1 The Great Fire of London was in 1666.
2 The plague, also known as the Black Death, killed thousands of people in London in 1348.
3 The seventeen hundreds is another way of saying the eighteenth century.
4 Many of London's buildings are Victorian, from the nineteenth century.
5 Elizabeth II became Queen in 1952.
6 London was called 'swinging London' in the sixties.
7 The Millennium Dome and the London Eye both opened in the year 2000.
8 The Olympic Games were held in London in 1948 and 2012.

4.2

V = Valerie Schroder, J = Jason Alvarez

1

V The vacation package was all-inclusive. It was great for a family resort. We had free children's entertainment, free drinks at the pool and a babysitter if we wanted to go out in the evening. But we were a little disappointed with the beach. The information pack said it was a private beach just for hotel guests but it was full of people and we had to pay extra to lie in the shade under a beach umbrella with sunbeds. It was also very hot in Cancún. Temperatures reached 104 degrees Fahrenheit – that's 40°C, and there weren't many palm trees on the beach! We would love to go again – but not in peak season.

2

J We stayed in Isla de Mujeres in Cancún, for our honeymoon. It is a fantastic island with beautiful, white, sandy beaches and there were lots of young couples like us. But it was very crowded, although it was quieter in the evening when all the day-trippers from Cancún left. We paid for half-board, not full-board – it was a tailored package. That way we could go on day trips and have lunch somewhere else. The package didn't include any sightseeing tours. We signed up for one to Xel-Ha, which is a kind of nature reserve with lagoons and caves. I guess it's OK for a family day out but we thought it was overpriced and too commercial for us. The best thing about the holiday was the snorkelling and seeing all the tropical fish. That was amazing, although we had to pay extra. Oh, and we could get the ferry to the mainland for free. It was a complimentary service for hotel guests staying on the island.

4.3

G = Guide, T1 = Tourist 1, T2 = Tourist 2

G Here we are! As you can see, the former bull ring was made into a shopping centre not very long ago. Plaza Arenas is now known as Arenas. We can visit the rooftop terrace at the end of the tour if we have time.

T1 Excuse me, who redesigned the bullring?
G That's a good question. The British architect, Richard Rogers, renovated it.
T1 So, the old bullring is now a shopping centre?
G That's right. Instead of bullfighting, you can go shopping, have some tapas, or watch a movie.
T1 Oh, great!
G The bull fights in Arenas stopped over 20 years ago. But if you're looking for some action, I recommend tomorrow's tour when we'll visit Barcelona's home football ground, Camp Nou.
T2 Do you mean the football stadium?
G That's right. Would you like to follow me now into the art gallery showing Romanesque art?
T1 What did he say?
T2 Sorry, did you say Roman Art?
G No, not Roman, Romanesque. It's the art style from the early Middle Ages. Right, let's go and see their collection of Romanesque Art. Can I have your art tickets please? Thanks, thank you.
T2 Oh, I don't have a ticket. He didn't give me a ticket, Gerhard.
T1 Yes, he did. Check your purse.

4.4

G = Guide, T1 = Tourist 1, T2 = Tourist 2

T1 Is it OK if I take a few photos?
G Sure, go ahead but no flash please.
T2 When did you say it was built?
G Ah, that's an interesting question. The basilica was completed in 1383. It only took 55 years to build, which was incredibly fast for Medieval times. It is the only example of a basilica built completely in the Catalan Gothic style. As I said earlier, the Santa Maria del Mar is my favourite religious building in Barcelona. As you can see it's very light, so you can really appreciate those beautiful stained glass windows. The windows aren't as old as the building and date from the 15th to 18th centuries. And did you know it was the inspiration for a best-selling novel by the Spanish writer, Idelfonso Falcones?
T2 Really?
G That's right.
T1 Excuse me, where is the restroom?
G I am afraid there aren't any toilets here. But you can go to a café nearby.
T1 Thanks, I really need to go.
T2 Ssh! Gerhard! You don't need to tell all of Barcelona!
G Here. Mind the step as you go. And now for the next question in our competition. When was this building completed? Was it the 12th, the 13th or the 14th century?

4.5

1

I really loved Austria, and our tour guides were friendly and helpful as they walked with us on the tour. We also got some useful tips about what to see and do in Salzburg. But our guide didn't seem to know that much about music. And I think there was too much walking for some of the older ones – some of the people in our group were very tired. I have to say, the package tour was rather expensive, especially with all the extra charges for some tickets and excursions. It wasn't all-inclusive as it said in the advert.

2

I'm new to the job as a tour guide, so I need to find out some more about Austrian composers before my next group. It would be a good idea to get some more training from the tour guide manager. My main criticism is that the company needs to be more transparent about prices. Many customers complained to me about the extra costs for some of the tickets and excursions – I had to say sorry but it wasn't my responsibility. And I'm sure we could offer packages that are more attractive for younger people.

3

Yes, the scenery was beautiful. But it wasn't organized so well. I mean, a six-day tour is too short for some of the older participants – they need more time to rest. And then the guide often disappeared to smoke! Once, the guide left us in Salzburg for an hour to spend money in local shops. I hate shopping! And we were really surprised when she told us after an evening concert that we had to take a taxi back to our hotel! That was another 18 euros we didn't plan to spend. The information we received said transfers were included but it was only airport transfers, so we were disappointed with the tour. It was overpriced and I won't be booking with Europa Cultural Tours again!

Unit 5

5.1

R = Receptionist, P = Mr Perry

R Good morning! Welcome to the Petrovskaya Hotel. How can I help you?
P Good morning! I have a reservation for three nights in the name of Perry.
R OK. May I have your passport, please?
P Here you are.
R Thank you, Mr Perry. Yes, you have a reservation for a double room for three nights. Is that correct?
P Yes, that's right.
R Could I have your credit card, please?
P OK.
R Thank you. Here is your key card. You are on the second floor and the room number is here.
P Thanks.
R Do you need any help with your luggage?
P No, thanks. I'll be fine. I'll take the lift.
R Enjoy your stay at the Petrovskaya Hotel, Mr Perry.

5.2

R = Receptionist, DG = Donald Golubkov, RG = Rachel Golubkov

R Good morning! Welcome to the Petrovskaya Hotel. How can I help you?
D Hi there! I'm Donald Golubkov and this is my wife, Rachel. We have a reservation.
R May I have your passports for a moment, please?
D Sure thing. Rachel, where did I put my passport?

RG Donnie, honey, I have them in my handbag, remember? Here you go.
R Thank you, Mr and Mrs Golubkov. Here are your passports. Your reservation is a double room with balcony for two nights. Your room rate doesn't include breakfast. Would you like breakfast in the morning?
D How much is it?
R Four hundred rubles per person.
RG What's that in dollars, Donnie?
D I have no idea but it sounds expensive to me. We'll pass on that one.
R Sorry?
RG That's a 'No' to breakfast.
R OK. Could I have your credit card, please?
D Sure.
R Thank you. Can you sign here, please? Here's your credit card. And here are your key cards and the room number is here. Your room is on the fifth floor.
D Thank you.
R Please remember to carry your key cards with you at all times. The security guard will ask to see them when you enter the hotel. Do you need any help with your luggage? Shall I call the porter?
D No, thank you. We only have these two suitcases.
RG Donnie, are you crazy, with your bad back? Yes, please, we'd like a porter.
R Certainly. My name is Nikolai, if there is anything we can do for you, please contact us at reception. Enjoy your stay at the Petrovskaya Hotel, Mr and Mrs Golubkov.
D Thank you. How do we get to our room?
R The lift is just over there, and the porter will show you to your room.

5.3

When I'm travelling on business, I don't usually spend much time in my hotel room. Even so, I want to have a comfortable place to sleep, shower and work. I need a fast Wi-Fi connection in my room and enough power outlets so I can charge my cell phones and laptop easily. Some chains now offer rooms with work desks, which is great. A voicemail service also makes my life easier, and the option to reserve a meeting room if I need to. Before I book a hotel for a business trip, I call them directly and ask if the hotel has any guest rooms specifically designed for business travellers. I expect the hotel to have a business centre which has equipment like a printer and a colour photocopier – and it's an enormous help if this has 24-hour access. I also want there to be someone available to provide technical support if there are any problems. 24-hour room service is a life saver when I've spent the whole day in meetings. The other essential is a good movie channel, so I can put my feet up and relax at the end of the day.

5.4

My needs are very different when I'm on holiday with the children. I'm divorced with a six-year-old daughter and a four-year-old son. If it's just the three of us on holiday together, I always like to go somewhere with a lot of attractions and facilities for the children, like a theme park or beach. I look for a hotel with a good-sized triple room and family facilities. The children are happy if there's a nice big outdoor swimming pool – preferably more than one. And a kids' club. It also gives me a chance to relax or read for a few hours during the day. I like to check before I book that the meal-times in the hotel are child-friendly and that the menu includes enough options for them. Oh, and a good laundry service is important, too, if we're staying for more than a few days. If my mother comes on holiday with us, we sometimes use the babysitting service and I take her out for dinner one night.

5.5

1
A What does it say on the website?
B It seems affordable. A single is US $95 in the summer season. A double is US $115, a triple is US $140 and a family room, for a maximum of four, costs US $170. We can save money if we share a room with my parents.
A Are you joking?

2
A I thought the shuttle from the airport to the hotel was a complimentary service but they charged us 20 euros per person.
B Really? I thought it was always free.
A Then, there was a bottle of water on the desk in the room. That cost us five euros when we checked out. And we also had to pay a six-euro tourist tax each, which we didn't know about.
B No way!
A Oh yes. Fortunately, I studied the hotel's list of telephone charges and used my mobile instead.

3
A I need to call Malaysia. What do I dial?
B From Europe you dial 0-0 and the country code, 0-6, and then the area or city code followed by the number you want.
A Hold on! I have to write this down. 0-0 and the country code, 0-6. The city code. I don't know that. What's the city code for Kuala Lumpur?
B Kuala Lumpur is three. So you dial 0-0, 0-6-3 and then the number.
A Got that. Great, thanks.

5.6

1
G = Guest, R = Receptionist
G Hello, we're checking out tomorrow and I just wanted to confirm our late checkout. We're in room 312.
R OK, let me just have a look. Oh, I'm afraid I don't have a record of a late checkout for you.
G Well, it mentions the option of a late checkout on your website and I requested it when I booked the room online. But I didn't get a reply.
R OK. Guests should really phone the hotel to ask for a late checkout.
G Well, it doesn't say that on your website. And I used the special requests box on the site.
R I understand. I'm sorry if the website isn't clear. Just a moment, let me see what I can do for you. I can let you have the room until 2 p.m.
G How much is that?
R There's no charge.
G Really? Lovely! Thank you very much for your help.
R You're welcome.

2
R = Receptionist, G = Guest
R Reception.
G Hello, this is Mr. Peterson in room 415. I just checked in.
R Yes.
G I asked for a room with a double bed but this room has twin beds.
R It's the same rate for a standard room.
G That's not the point. I'd like a double room not a twin room – that's what I booked. And there's another thing. I expected a nicer room than this for my money.
R What's wrong with the room?
G Well, let's see. The furniture is old and shabby, the towels are hard and paper thin, the light switch is broken and there's no hot water in the bathroom.
G Hello, are you still there?
R Yes.
G Well, what are you going to do about this?
R You want fresh towels?
G Towels! Are you listening to me?
R Yes, yes. I'll send someone from maintenance to check the water and the light switch.
G No, no, I want a double room.
R There are no double rooms available. We're fully booked this weekend.
G Well, why didn't you say that earlier? Look, I'm coming down to talk to your manager.

5.7

1

Most European guests are happy with the room sizes. It's usually the North Americans and Australians who expect bigger rooms. We should offer guests an upgrade to a junior suite on check-in if one is available. It's only another 10 euros and the room is twice the size. Also, we should email in advance and tell families what to expect if they want to put a child's cot in the standard rooms.

2

Lots of guests arrive for weekend breaks on a Friday evening on low-cost flights from all over Europe. We should check the flight arrival times and make sure there are enough staff on reception when there is a busy period like that. Otherwise guests get frustrated and impatient.

3

We had a few very busy nights in the restaurant last month when some waiting staff were off sick and we had two new members of the team. They were obviously slower than the others and forgot to serve one or two customers. The duty manager didn't phone me to tell me the situation. We should have a list of staff phone numbers to call people who are off duty in cases of emergency like that. The café staff do a good job but one or two of them don't speak very good English and they are a bit shy around the guests for that reason.

4

The majority of our guests know what to expect when they come to the hotel. They love the fact that we are a 'green' hotel and they understand why we don't have some equipment in the rooms and why we use smaller towels. Some guests are unhappy that they have to come to reception to ask for shower gel and shampoo. But I don't think we should change things.

Unit 6

6.1

S = Shop Assistant, C1 = Customer 1, C2 = Customer 2

S: Next, please.
C1 Hi, we'd like to order some sandwiches.
S: Sure. To eat in or take away?
C1 To take away. I'd like a chicken sandwich.
C2 And cheese and tomato for me, please.
S OK. Would you like sliced bread or a baguette? The baguettes are freshly made.
C1 OK, I'll have the baguette.
C2 Sliced bread for me. Do you have brown bread?
S Yes, we do. So that's a chicken baguette and a cheese and tomato sandwich on brown bread. Would you like any extra fillings?
C1 Yes, please. Can I have some salad in the baguette?
S OK. Would you like some homemade soup with that? Today's soup is chicken and mushroom.
C2 Sounds tasty. Yes, please.
C1 Not for me. Thanks.
S: And what would you like to drink with that?
C1 A bottle of sparkling water for me, please.
C2 I'll have a coffee. Do you do decaf?
S Yes, we do. Regular or large?
C2 Regular will be fine.
S Would you like some desserts? We have a great selection of homemade cakes and muffins.
C1 Those do look appetizing. I think I'll have a blueberry muffin.
C2 And me. No, make mine a chocolate brownie.
S Would you like to pay for that together or separately?
C1 Together.
C2 Separately.
C1 No, I'll get this one, Claudette. My treat.
C2 OK, thanks very much.
C1 Together, please.
S So that's fifteen euros fifty altogether, please.
C1 Here you are.
S That's four fifty change. I'll just get your order ready for you.

6.2

S = Sandra Kellerman, H = Henry Martins
S Hello, Sandra Kellerman speaking.
H Hi, Sandra. It's Henry Martins from P&K Sports here.
S Henry! Good to hear from you.
H Listen, we're organizing a big marketing event next month, on the 25th of June. We're expecting a lot of people, and we need some food – a buffet. Can you do the catering?
S The 25th. Yeah, sure. Just give me some details. How many guests are you expecting?
H We're not sure yet. We sent out 1,500 invitations and there are about 300 employees here.
S So that's around 1,800. I know it's impossible to get an exact number but can you confirm the guest numbers a week before, say on the 17th?
H OK. How much will it cost? Can you give me an estimate?
S Well, it depends on what kind of buffet you want. Is it breakfast, lunchtime, or dinner? Is it formal or informal?
H It's an evening event but the plan is to be very casual and relaxed.
S I see. Would you like some menu options? Then you can see the price per head and make your selection.
H Yes, great! You have my email, don't you?
S Yeah. I'll send them to you today. What's the location for the event?
H We've hired Marley's Golf Club.
S Good. I know the place. There's a lot of space there. I'll need to visit the club to see how we can organize the buffet stations. Will they do the drinks?
H Yes, that's right. Sorry, forgot to mention that.
S So you don't need any beverages?
H No. I mean, yes. We'd like some tea and coffee. You know, some hot beverages.
S OK. And how much time do we have to prepare the buffet and clean up after?
H Good question. Listen, I have an idea. Let's visit the golf club together and we can discuss it with the club manager.
S Good idea. Let's see, I'm available on …

6.3

1

The seafood salad comes with a creamy, lemon dressing made with olive oil, vinegar, yoghurt, mayonnaise, mustard and fresh lemons.

2

Our Florentine steak is seasoned with sea salt and black pepper, and served with white beans.

3

Try our tasty beef Milanese. It's coated in egg and breadcrumbs, and then fried.

4

The chicken is marinated in lemon juice, olive oil and garlic for 24 hours, and then barbecued.

6.4

A In the USA the first part of a meal, or the first course, is the appetizer. It's a small dish of food before the main meal. You know, perhaps some salad or soup, or a small pasta dish.
B Appetizer? Really? In the UK we usually say that's the starter. What about the main part of the meal? We call that the main course.
A Yeah, in the USA we can say the main course or the entrée. And people sometimes ask for side orders with the entrée. These come on separate plates and are usually extra potatoes or vegetables, or a side salad.
B Yes, that's more or less the same in the UK. Is the sweet course at the end of the meal called the dessert?
A That's right. We use the same word for that.

6.5

W = Waiter, C1 = Customer 1, C2 = Customer 2
W Are you ready to order?
C1 Well, yes, nearly. We just have a few questions about the menu. What kind of sauce does the seafood salad come with?
W I believe the dressing is made with olive oil, vinegar, yoghurt, mayonnaise, mustard and fresh lemon.
C1 Sounds delicious. Could I have the dressing on the side?
W On the side?
C1 Yes, on a separate plate.
W Well, it's usual to serve the dressing with the salad.
C1 I understand. It's just that I'm a diabetic and I have to watch my cholesterol and fat levels.
W Of course, madam. I'll make a note for the chef. And for you, sir?
C2 I'll have the chilli prawns. Oh, hold on, is there garlic in that?
W Yes, the prawns are fried with lemon, chilli and garlic.
C2 No garlic for me, thanks.
W And for the main course?
C2 What's beef Milanese?
W It's beef coated in egg and breadcrumbs, and then fried.
C2 Have you got any meat that isn't covered in sauce or breadcrumbs?
W I suggest you try the Bistecca Alla Fiorentina or Florentine steak. It's a popular dish in Tuscany, cooked in the most simple way possible, with a little olive oil and seasoned with sea salt and lots of black pepper, then grilled to a medium rare perfection.
C2 That's exactly what I want. What does it come with?
W It's served with white beans.
C2 Not for me thanks. I'm a meat and potato man. Can I have a side order of fries?
W Sorry?
C2 A plate of fries with my steak.
W We don't usually … I'll see what we can do. And for you, madam?
C1 I see the tuna steak comes in a tomato sauce. Would it be possible not to put any salt in the sauce?
W I'm afraid the sauce is already prepared, madam. You could order the tuna without the sauce, and I'll make a note of your request for no salt with your fish.
C1 Thank you.

6.6

C = Consultant, R = Restaurant Owner

C Well, now let's look at why the sales are low this year. I think the first problem is the menu.

R What's wrong with the menu? It's always been popular in the past.

C Yes, I know. But I'd cut some of the meat dishes.

R But meat is the central concept of our restaurant.

C Yes, I'm not saying don't have any meat dishes but people's tastes are changing.

R I see.

C Another point is the décor and lighting. It's quite old-fashioned and dark. You know, it's usually the woman who decides where to eat these days and a fresher, brighter look would attract more customers.

R A new décor you say. Sounds expensive.

C It doesn't have to be. I've seen some lovely bistro restaurants with second-hand tables and chairs. Now let's look at some other opportunities you have to attract more customers. I see you don't have a set menu at lunchtime. I also think that your portions are big and customers often leave food on the plate. You could reduce the portion sizes and waste, to reduce costs.

R Yes, I suppose that would help to sell more desserts.

C You should also consider special diets and introduce more healthy options. I mean, just one vegetarian dish on the menu isn't enough.

R But it doesn't sell very well.

C True. But that's probably because a veggie burger isn't very appetizing and this is a meat restaurant. If you have more seafood and vegetables dishes, you can change the concept a little and attract a new type of customer. Have maybe one or two things on the menu indicated as vegetarian or suitable for diabetics, or low-calorie. People love that.

R OK. I'll have to think about it.

C So, what are the threats to your business?

R A big one is the fluctuating food prices. Meat is getting very expensive, especially lamb.

C Yes, that's true. Another good reason to have fewer meat options. And there is also a changing attitude to food and eating out. People expect something more ethnic these days. I think a few Mediterranean or Asian dishes on your menu would be really popular. Try some fusion cooking.

R Yes, maybe. I like Thai grilled beef salad myself.

Unit 7

7.1

T = Tour Director, T1 = Tourist 1

Part One

T OK, folks listen up. Here's some information about our itinerary. We're leaving San José at 6 a.m. tomorrow.

T1 Six o'clock!

T Yeah, it's bright and early. We're flying south to Quepos and we're staying in a small jungle lodge near there for three nights. We're going to spend tomorrow at Parque Nacional Manuel Antonio on the Pacific coast. There is lots of wildlife to see there. Remember you'll want to wear a bathing suit and bring a towel – the park's magnificent beaches are perfect for swimming and sunbathing. And a word of warning – don't feed the monkeys.

On day three you have a choice of two tours from Boca Damas: a horseback ride with a local nature guide to Tocori Waterfall, or kayaking along the coast. This tour includes a snorkelling break.

On day four we're heading north to the Rainmaker Conservation Project. Again there are two options: a gentle forest walk to a river where you can swim, or the nature trail complete with suspension bridges between the treetops – a perfect place to spot the wildlife and learn about the rainforest from the local guide.

7.2

Part Two

T = Tour Director, T2 = Tourist 2, T3 = Tourist 3

T On day five we're going to drive a short distance along Highway 34 to Jacó for a three-night stay in a nature lodge near there. From there we're taking the Pacific Rainforest aerial tram. That's a ride through the treetops on open-air gondolas. You'll get some fabulous views of the Pacific coast from there.

We're going further up Highway 34 the next day to Tárcoles where we're taking a boat safari from the village up the river Tárcoles to see the crocodiles. Keep your hands inside the boat because these reptiles can get very close.

T2 Are there many of them?

T Oh, yes. I'm sure you'll see a lot of crocodiles. People have counted more than two hundred in a kilometre and a half.

T3 Wow!

T On day seven we're going to visit Parque Nacional Carara with some of the most varied forests and wildlife in Costa Rica. On day eight, you have the morning free to explore Jacó, take a surfing lesson, go shopping for souvenirs, or simply relax. In the afternoon, we're flying back to San José from Jacó airport for the last two nights of this tour. I'm sure you'll have lots of fun. Any questions so far about the itinerary?

7.3

1

Victoria Falls or Mosi-oa-Tunya is the largest waterfall in the world. It is located in southern Africa on the Zambezi River between the countries of Zambia and Zimbabwe. The falls are 108 m high and 1.7 km wide.

2

The Fish River Canyon is located in the south of Namibia. It is the second largest canyon in the world and the largest in Africa. The canyon is 160 km long, up to 27 km wide and almost 550 m deep in places.

7.4

Part One

Good morning, everyone! I'm Janusz Karpowicz from the northeast Poland Tourism Association and I'd like to talk to you about Poland's best kept secret. So to start with, I'd like to ask you all a question. Have you ever heard of the land of a thousand lakes? Where do you think it is? Poland? That's right. In Polish we call it the Mazury and we think it's the most beautiful lakeland area in Europe. Today I want to tell you about a very special nature resort. It's the stunningly beautiful Masuria Paradise in northeast Poland. So why is the Masuria Paradise resort unique? One of the reasons is our guest accommodation, which is not like anything else in the region. Our visitors stay in traditional wooden lodges built around a small lake with spectacular views across the water and surrounding forests. We offer an amazing range of water sports including canoeing, sailing and swimming – the lake has a swimming area that's also safe for children. There are also outdoor activities such as cycling, bird-watching, tours of the local nature reserves, or mushroom-picking in the forest. Out of high season we also organize conferences and receive specialist groups, for example, bird-watching enthusiasts, or companies on training courses. We specialize in team-building activities including sailing courses, archery competitions and horse-riding. As well as daytime activities, we also offer our guests a programme of evening entertainment including concerts in our popular underground café. We have regular barbecues and guests take part in singing by the campfire under the stars. When you visit, I'm sure you will agree our nature resort is an undiscovered paradise in Poland. Thank you for your attention. Right, I'll be happy to take any questions now.

7.5

Part Two

J = Janusz Karpowicz, T1 = Tourist 1, T2 = Tourist 2, T3 = Tourist 3

J OK, so does anyone have any questions? Yes?

T1 How far are you from the nearest town?

J We're about 10 km from the nearest village. But we can arrange minibus transfers from other towns.

T2 Can guests use their mobile phones in the area?

J Guests can't use their mobile phones in the forest. But we have phones in the main building. We usually find people come to Masuria Paradise to get away from work and the city.

T3 You say Masuria Paradise is a nature resort. In what ways?

J Well, basically, we offer simple accommodation in unspoiled countryside. We also have food that is locally sourced, erm, local food, whenever possible, on our menu. And we are respectful of the environment. And you won't find motorboats on the lake compared to some of the bigger lakes in the region. We are pleased to have accreditation from the European Association for Nature Tourism and we make an effort to keep to its standards.

T1 You say you're organizing an open day for tourism professionals. When is it?

J Oh yes, good question. It's the first weekend of next month. If you leave me your email addresses, I'll send you the details. Well, if there are no more questions, please feel free to take a copy of our brochure and my card.

7.6

1

C = Customer, P = Professional

C We like the people at Wero. Your staff are really helpful and friendly but we'd like to do something more adventurous this year. So we're thinking of booking with Manu Adventures. They can offer us bungee jumping, flightseeing and hot air ballooning. I mean, we can go tramping and mountain biking any time. Wero's activities are a bit too easy and a bit boring, to be honest.

P OK, thank you. Could you tell me, is your group interested in water sports like jet boating and skurfing?

C Skurfing? That's a mix of water skiing and surfing, isn't it?

P Yes, it's very popular on rivers.

C It sounds fun. But we don't want anything too expensive. We need to be realistic about costs.

P Yes, I see Manu Adventures charge high prices for their packages.

C Yes. But they include a lot of different activities.

2

C = Customer, P = Professional

C The equipment was fine for the activities. But why don't you offer more extreme water sports like jet boating and skurfing?

P That's a good idea. What about SNUBA® diving?

C SNUBA® diving?

P It's like scuba diving but the divers breathe through a long tube which is connected to a scuba oxygen tank. There is no heavy diving equipment and you are never far from the boat with the oxygen.

C Sounds interesting. Do you need to be very sporty to do it?

P Not especially. It's great for beginners and older people. Was there anything else you'd like to tell us?

C Just that we'd like to try jet boating, skurfing and SNUBA® diving next time. And I think you should have discounts for large groups.

P Discounts for groups. I see. Well, thanks very much for your feedback.

3

C = Customer, P = Professional

C Some of the equipment was old and not safe. And, although our instructor was really friendly and a great person, he wasn't very enthusiastic. I think you need some younger, more energetic staff.

P Oh, OK. Anything else?

C Yes, you should offer more exciting activities like glacier trekking, flightseeing, or jet boating.

P I see.

C And your price list doesn't include the additional insurance for some of the activities, like for white-water rafting. It's not good to find out about things at the last minute. You should clearly mark extra charges in your prices.

P That's been very helpful. Thanks.

Unit 8

8.1

Heathrow is one of the world's busiest airports. There are over thirteen hundred flights a day, carrying on average 190,000 passengers. Heathrow deals with nearly 69 million arriving and departing passengers every year. And most incredible of all, Heathrow has only two runways for almost half a million flights a year, making it the busiest international air space in the world.

8.2

1

A Terminal 4 departures. €35.50 please.

B How much?

A €35.50, sir.

B But the meter says €31.00.

A There is a supplement of €4.50 on the fare to and from the airport.

B Oh, I see. Can I have a receipt, please?

A Certainly.

2

A Can I have your passport and boarding pass, please?

B Yes, here you are.

A Do you have any baggage to check in?

B Yes, please. This suitcase. Can I take two carry-on bags?

A I'm afraid passengers are only allowed one piece of hand baggage plus a laptop or handbag.

B OK. So I'll check the big bag and take this one with me on board.

A Do you have any liquids or sharp objects in your hand baggage?

B Erm … Oh, yes, I do.

A Well, you have plenty of time before your flight if you want to repack your cases.

B Repack? What, here on the terminal floor?

A Yes, you can go just over there.

B OK, I'll do that. Where did you say?

A Just over there on your right.

3

A Please remove your coats and jackets, belts, watches, jewellery, mobile phones, keys and metal items, and put all items in a tray for X-ray. Excuse me, sir, are you carrying a laptop in that bag?

B Umm, yes.

A Can you take it out of the bag and put it in a tray to go through the X-ray machine?

B Sure.

A OK, sir. Can you walk through the metal detector?

B It's my knee. It happens every time I go through security. I had an operation and there's a metal plate in my knee, you see.

A OK, could you step over here, please?

8.3

1

A Excuse me, where's the nearest restroom?

B Restroom? Ah, yes, the toilets. Go right here. Then go straight on past the check-in desks. When you get to the end, turn left. They are on the right just after the lifts. I mean elevators.

A So, that's past the check-in counters, and turn left and they're on the right?

B That's right.

A Thank you.

2

A Is this the Tourist Information Office?

B No, this is the Airport Information Desk. If you want Tourist Information, you should go across the terminal, past the café and the airline offices, and then turn right. It's on the left between the car rental offices and the hotel reservation desk.

A So it's at the other end of the building, between the car hire offices and hotel reservations.

B Yes.

3

A How do I get to the departure gates? I'm in a hurry.

B You need to go right here, past the check-in desks. Then take the escalators or the lift to the first floor to go through security. Then follow the signs for your gate number.

A Cheers.

4

A Excuse me, which way to the airport bus?

B Go through the exit door on the left and turn right. You'll see the bus stop just outside the terminal building.

A Thanks a lot.

8.4

I = Interviewer, A = Air Traffic Controller

I Which airport do you work at, Santiago?

A Actually, I don't work at an airport. I work at an Area Control Centre.

I I see, so you don't work in an airport control tower and you don't see the planes?

A That's right. You see, air traffic control is divided into a number of different jobs. The job of the controllers who work at airports is to help the pilots during take-off, as they fly the planes out of the airport, and during landing, when they arrive. At peak times, there is a lot of traffic at big international airports and airport terminal controllers are responsible for directing all this. They coordinate all the different take-off and landing times, make sure that the aircraft have enough room to manoeuvre and that there is a safe distance between them. The en route, or area controllers, like me, help to guide the pilots and direct air traffic flow between airports. We use radar and computer systems to follow the exact position of each aircraft in flight.

8.5

1

F = Flight attendant, P1 = Passenger 1, P2 = Passenger 2

F Hello guys, is everything all right? Are you enjoying the flight?

P1 Yeah, sure. We're having a great time.

F That's good. Listen, could you keep the noise down a bit?

P2 Why? Who's complaining?

F It's just that you are a big group and you are making a lot of noise. We can hear you all over the plane. It might disturb the other passengers.

P1 OK. Guys, guys keep it down a bit. Can I use the toilet?

F I am afraid the 'fasten seat belt' sign is on now. You see, we are descending into Madrid soon.

P1 Oh dear, it's just that I'm a bit desperate.

F It won't be long before we land.

P1 Right. Well then, I'll just have to wait.

F Thank you. Enjoy yourselves in Madrid.

2

F = Flight attendant,
A = Announcement, P = Passenger

P Oh, what's that? What's that? What's happening? Why's the plane shaking like that? What's that noise?

A Ladies and gentlemen, the pilot has switched on the 'fasten seatbelt' sign. Please return to your seats and fasten your seat belts until the sign is switched off.

P Excuse me … Excuse me, what's happening?

F We're just passing through an area of turbulence. Don't worry, it's perfectly normal.

A Cabin crew, please take your seats.

P Oh, no! Oh no, we're all going to die!

F Please rest assured everything is fine. The turbulence will be over in a few minutes. In the meantime, just remain seated with your seatbelt fastened. We'll continue the food and drink service when the 'fasten seat belt' sign is switched off.

3

F = Flight attendant, P = Passenger

F Please have your passport and boarding passes ready for … Excuse me, sir. I'm afraid that suitcase is too big to take on board.

P What?

F I'm sorry, that suitcase is too big to take on board as hand baggage.

P But I always take this bag on the plane.

F I'm afraid we have a full flight today and we have to be strict about the allowance.

P Don't be ridiculous.

F I'm sorry but we'll have to check your bag in here at the boarding gate.

P Well, I'm not at all happy about this.

F That will be €45, please.

P What? No way! I don't believe this! You're going to charge me?

F Yes, there is a charge.

P But my ticket only cost me €60. This is totally unacceptable. You people, you overcharge, you lie, you …

F Look, the airline's regulations are very clear – if you don't pay to check in your baggage online, you have to pay a fee of €30 at check-in. And at the boarding gate it increases to €45. Right?

P This is outrageous! I'm going to complain about this.

F Yes sir. Please stop shouting at me – it doesn't help. You can send any comments and complaints via our web page. Thank you.

P I want to speak to your supervisor right now.

Unit 9

9.1

R = Ray, M = Matilda

R Hello, Matilda, isn't it? How are you today?

M Fine, Mr Kavanagh.

R Oh, call me Ray. Have you done all the rooms on the third floor yet?

M No, I haven't. I've just finished room 303.

R 303! That means you haven't done the other seven rooms yet!

M No, Mr Kavanagh. I mean, Ray.

R Never mind. I know it's your first week. I'll ask Maureen to help, OK?

M Thanks.

R Let me check this room first. Let's see. Look, you've missed a bit here on the mirror. And the toiletries go on the right, just so!

M Sorry.

R Not to worry. Practice makes perfect! Oh dear, I'm afraid the floor is not up to standard. See, you haven't done the corners very well. Could you go over those again, please?

M Sure.

R And have you checked the number of towels, linen, and clothes hangers?

M The hangers? I thought they were anti-theft ones, ones the guests can't steal.

R Yes, they are but we still need to count them. The number of things that disappear from our rooms! Oh, look the guests have left you a tip. I've already explained our tipping system, haven't I, Matilda?

M No, I don't think so.

R Well, we always share the tips at the end of a shift.

M We share the tips?

R That's right, between all the housekeepers. I'll take this for now, all right? And I'll go and see if Maureen has finished her rooms yet.

M That was $20.

R And remember, we've got a group checking in at 2 p.m. So, hurry, hurry! We haven't got all day!

M Yes, Mr Kavanagh.

9.2

I = Interviewer, D = Davis Langdon

I Today I'm talking to Davis Langdon, expert in hotel refurbishment. Mr Langdon, why is refurbishment important?

D Hotels need to refurbish regularly to maintain customer loyalty, or room rates and stay competitive. There are basically two types of refurbishment, depending on the work done: refreshment and complete remodelling.

I How often do hotels usually refresh rooms? And why?

D Hoteliers typically refresh every five to seven years. Perhaps they need to add new fittings, or make changes to rooms to make sure the hotel stays competitive. This can mean replacing furniture like beds, chairs and bedside tables, fittings in bathrooms like taps or shower screens, or installing new lighting. But it can simply be changing door sizes, making doors bigger to accommodate larger trolleys.

I I see, and what about more major work for a hotel?

D Well, when a hotel wants to upgrade or increase room rates, or the number of guests, it will change complete guest floors.

I You mean, replace bathrooms, or extend the hotel and build new guest rooms?

D That's right. Hoteliers sometimes want to add air conditioning, or introduce modern facilities, for example, IT services and in-room entertainment, like flat screen TVs.

I And what about customer expectations? What changes have we seen?

D Well, we've seen a lot of innovations in the business and luxury sectors. Boutique hotels have set new standards in interior decoration, especially for younger guests. Customers today are attracted to stylish design or services, such as pools and spas and conference facilities for corporate guests.

9.3

R = Receptionist, S = Susan Meyer,
P = Pieter Meyer

R Good morning, Mrs Meyer. How may I help you?

S I'd like to check out please. I asked for the bill yesterday evening but I have a couple of questions.

R Yes, of course.

S Could you tell me what this charge is here for €80.50?

R That's the cost of a third person in your room, for your daughter.

S But I thought you charged a different rate for children under 12?

R That's right. It's minus thirty percent, so we've only charged €281.75.

S And what are the €30 for? It says cafeteria but we only had a couple of coffees and some ice creams one day. It should be ten euros, not 30.

R Let me check our records for the cafeteria. Ah, I have receipts for ice creams and drinks from the 30th, the 31st, and the 2nd.

S Oh. Pieter, do you know anything about this? Did you have ice creams and drinks without me on two days?

P Uh, yes, I think we did a couple of times.

S OK, sorry about that. But we definitely didn't have any orange juice in the restaurant on the 31st. I remember we ordered some fresh juice and then changed our minds.

R I'll just check. Yes, there seems to have been a mistake there. I do apologize about that, Mrs Meyer.

S That's OK.

R Do you have any other questions?

S The seven percent is VAT, isn't it?

R Yes, and VAT is already included in the price. The total amount is now ten euros 50 less. And the total amount should now be €1,182.25.

S And I paid 20% when I booked.

R Exactly. So the balance due is now €964.90. I'll print a new folio for you.

S Thanks.

9.4

R = Receptionist, S = Susan Meyer

R OK, so you'd like to check out now. Will you be paying with the same credit card?

S Yes.

R Could you enter your pin number here? How was your stay with us?

S Great. And we loved the food – the new chef is excellent!

R I'm glad to hear it. Here's your receipt.

S Thank you. Has our taxi arrived yet?

R No, not yet. It'll be about five minutes. Do you need assistance with your luggage?

S No, thanks, we're fine.

R Thank you for staying with us, Mrs Meyer. We hope to see you again soon. Have a good journey!

All Bye/Adiós!

9.5

C1 = Contractor 1, E = Emilio

C1 Clean and Sheen. How can I help you?

E Hi. We're interested in contracting you for a big post-refurbishment cleaning job. Would you be able to give us a quotation?

C1 Yes, we're experienced in post-refurbishment cleaning. I need to ask you some questions first. How big is the hotel?

E We have 52 suites and 24 apartments.

C1 Have they all been refurbished?

E No, just the 52 suites.

C1 And what about the public areas?

E There's the restaurant, bar, pool and new spa, and the hotel lobby of course.

C1 Spa and lobby, I see.

E Can I ask what type of products you use? Do you use any chemical agents?

C1 No, we make sure that all our products are environmentally friendly, for example, for window cleaning we use purified water. And we always use the latest equipment and modern methods like pressure washing.

E Sounds good. Can you give me a quotation?

C1 Well, our standard rate is about $15 per hour.

E And how long will the clean-up take?

C1 Ah, that depends on the number of floors, if there are many stairs, and the size of the areas. How much time have you allocated for cleaning?

E About three days.

C1 I see. We usually recommend one week for a big clean up operation. And when is this for?

E It's for next week.

C1 Would you like us to send someone over tomorrow morning for a consultation?

E Great.

C1 What about 9 a.m.?

E Nine in the morning? Yes, that's fine.

9.6

C2 = Contractor 2, E = Emilio

C2 Cleaning on Wheels.

E Hi, it's Emilio Méndez here calling from the Devonshire Hotel. I'd like to ask you a few questions about the clean-up job we exchanged emails about.

C2 Yes, of course.

E First, have Cleaning on Wheels ever done a job like this before? You're a small company.

C2 Yes, of course, lots of times. We're the best in New Hampshire! Didn't my brother Evan tell you?

E Evan, our new front desk clerk? Yes, he recommended you. But I have a few more questions for you, Ms. …?

C2 Tracy, just call me Tracy.

E So, Tracy, what type of cleaning products do you use? Do you use chemical agents?

C2 Well, we use all the well-known brands of course. But we try not to use too much bleach or anything too strong.

E And how much will it cost for a clean-up? Can you give me a quotation?

C2 Well, we charge by the hour and the rate is $12 an hour. But if it's a big job, I'm sure we can come to an agreement.

E That sounds reasonable. And how long do you think you would take?

C2 It depends, Emilio. If you have four cleaners working eight hours a day, that'll cost you 384 for an eight-hour day. But I could organize two teams with two shifts a day – that'll be faster.

E I see. Well, we've allocated three days before reopening.

C2 Three days? No problem. Evan tells me this is for next week, right?

E Yes, as soon as possible.

C2 Listen, why don't I come by at 4 p.m. and check out the surfaces and windows.

E Today? Yes, that's fine. See you at four then.

Unit 10

10.1

1

I work for the local tourist office. At the moment I'm giving out flyers for a South Korean folk village. The village has 260 traditional houses of the Joseon Dynasty. Visitors can see how South Koreans ate, dressed and lived in the past. You can see handicrafts like pottery, baskets and bamboo products. It's a good way to get to know our culture and customs. There's music, dance, acrobats, a traditional wedding and a tea ceremony. Only costs 15,000 won. Take the bus in front of Suweon Station. Here, take a leaflet.

2

I work in the marketing department for a four-star hotel in Seoul. Visitors love Seoul because it is a mix of the old and new: there are temples, palaces and pagodas but also modern skyscrapers and neon lights. We have a lot of business guests because South Korea is a centre of finance and many international corporations have their headquarters here. What do I do in my department? I discuss ideas for promotions with the marketing team, for example, electronic postcards of the hotel, online promotions, like discounts for business travellers. I also have to work with a team of designers, website designers and translators to produce our marketing material in Chinese, English

and other languages. The desk clerks mention my name when guests check in. But visitors usually want to go directly up to their room when they arrive, so it's best to talk to them during their stay. This means I sometimes sit in the hotel lobby and tell guests about our special deals, promotions like four nights for the price of three for advanced bookings, you know, to encourage return guests. That's what you call 'upselling'.

3

I work for an international marketing agency. We're currently working with the Tourist Board of South Korea. We're creating a new, exciting campaign promoting South Korea to tourists and foreign investors. The slogan of the last campaign was 'Korea: be inspired'. How do we create a marketing campaign? Well, we have brainstorming meetings, and we choose the best ideas, then we work on the marketing plan and turn our ideas into reality. We will write a script for the TV commercial, and organize interactive screens in shopping malls or perhaps outdoor advertising on the subway. Before, we usually placed print advertisements in business newspapers and magazines. But nowadays we can create more interest with online videos and social media, like Facebook and tweets.

10.2

1 The Wi-Fi situation in hotels drives me crazy and when they charge for hidden extras, such as using the gym or other resort facilities. If luxury hotels continue to charge ten dollars for Wi-Fi, they'll lose guests, especially business guests. Travellers want value for their money and most mid-priced hotels don't charge for Wi-Fi.

2 In the next ten years the airline industry is probably going to make 35 percent of their sales from extra charges. I don't think they're going to give up charges like baggage fees. But I hate it when airlines promote one price to customers, then charge a different, higher price when you book your flight. And if low-cost carriers charge for using the restroom or toilet on flights, other airlines will probably do the same.

3 I think if solo travel becomes more popular, cruises and hotels will stop charging single supplements. There's a huge market for baby boomers, especially older women who are on their own but want to get out and do things. River cruising in Germany and Austria is going to be a big thing in the future. It's a very safe way for single women to travel.

4 60% of our magazine readers used a travel agent last year, which surprised me. People will go back to using travel agents if there is too much information online. Travel is getting harder in many ways, and travel agents are here to help you. I think it's a sort of travel therapy.

5 The key word in travel these days is experiential marketing. Travel is all about the experience – something

that's authentic and not everyday. Travellers are becoming more interested in very specific things, like food, art, family history, or bird-watching. If consumers have more specific interests, tourism organizations won't be able to sell general packages. Packages will become more tailored and customized.

6 Nowadays there are so many ways to get travel information, and everything is going digital. My colleagues think we should do more online video but I don't agree. Most people don't click on travel videos when they look at websites at work. Either they don't want their boss to know they're using the internet, or they can't watch videos in the office.

10.3

1 If there is a natural disaster, the airports will close.
2 If the airports close, airlines will cancel flights.
3 If airlines cancel flights, passengers won't be able to travel.
4 If passengers aren't able to travel, they will complain.
5 If passengers complain, the airlines will pay passengers compensation.
6 If airlines pay passengers compensation, they will lose money.
7 If airlines lose money, they will increase their prices.
8 If they increase their prices, people will probably fly less.

10.4

C = Carpet dealer, T1 = Tourist 1, T2 = Tourist 2

C Do you want a Turkish carpet? Best prices in Istanbul!
T1 What about that one, that rug there?
C Ah, this is a quality kilim, a traditional Turkish rug. This is very high quality and handmade. Look, you can see the special marking on the back. Can I ask, are you from London?
T1 No, Liverpool, up north.
C Ah, Liverpool has a great football team.
T1 It certainly has.
C This kilim is the very best traditional craftsmanship. I don't have many left, so I can give you a special price.
T1 OK, how much is it?
C 250 TRY.
T1 250 TRY? Um, that's about 88 pounds. No, sorry, that's too much for me.
C You won't find a kilim of this quality anywhere else in the market for so little.
T1 What if I give you 150 TRY for it?
C Tsk, tsk.
T1 I've seen one like this in a shop for 150 TRY.
C Tsk. Imitation probably.
T1 I'll give you 180 TRY for it.
C What about these cushions? One kilim and two cushions for 220 TRY.
T1 220 TRY?
T2 Andy!
T1 He wants 220 TRY for the rug and cushions.
T2 But we haven't got that much cash. Let's go.

C No lira, no problem. We take euros or pounds. Your husband is buying a beautiful kilim for you!
T1 But look at the colours, Christine – it really is a beautiful piece of work.
C Tell your friends to come to the Grand Bazaar and I'll give them a discount, 10 percent. And I can give you a special extra discount on the rug and cushions – 200 TRY for the lot.
T1 OK.
T2 Andy! If you pay him, I won't have enough cash to buy a handbag!
C Ah, if you want a bag, go to my cousin, Zeki over there. He sells very nice bags, at a good price too.

10.5

B = Bodrum resort representative, V = Vassili

B We are impressed with your CV, Vassili and you have been successful at the assessment centre. So, I'm happy to tell you, you can start with us on Monday. Report to me at eight o'clock and I'll introduce you to the other holiday reps in the Bodrum resort. Any questions?
V Yes. We haven't talked about the salary yet.
B Yes. It's 1,700 TRY per month. Living accommodation and the uniform is included, plus a free flight home once a year.
V Sounds good. But doesn't the company pay for two flights every year?
B It depends. For you it's one flight.
V Really? My friend Dmitri said he had two free flights this year.
B Ah, yes. It's different with Dmitri. He's an experienced rep who has worked for us for three years. He recommended you. If you work well, and we're happy with you, we'll talk about it next year, OK? Don't forget, you get a food allowance too.
V Oh, of course. Thank you. I'm happy to start on Monday, sir.
B Good, good. Now, if you come with me, we'll have some mint tea and I'll show you where you need to go on Monday.

10.6

T = Tourist, A = Attendent

T Hello, we'd like two loungers and a parasol, please.
A Two loungers and one parasol? But there are four of you.
T Yes, but two of us can lie on the beach.
A Tsk. Sorry, that's not possible. This area is for loungers only.
T Oh, I see. Maybe tomorrow.
A Wait a minute. Perhaps I can give you a special offer, because it's almost four. Four loungers for the price of three.
T Four for the price of three? What about the parasol?
A The umbrellas are extra. If you want four loungers, you'll need two umbrellas. That's 22 TRY all together.
T No, sorry.
A Tell me, where are you staying in Bodrum?
T At the Hotel Ephesus.

A Oh yes? I have friends there. Listen, I'll make you a special deal, because you're from Hotel Ephesus. Four loungers for the price of three, and I won't charge for the second umbrella. So that's only fourteen TRY. How does that sound?
T OK, great. 14 TRY.
A Enjoy your stay in Bodrum!

10.7

Bangkok and beaches. That's what most people think when you mention Thailand. Most Asian visitors to Thailand stay in Bangkok. Whilst most Western tourists visit Bangkok but also Thailand's beautiful beaches in the south and resorts like Phuket, Krabi and Pattaya. However, the northeast of Thailand, known as Isan, has a fascinating, unique culture. Isan is situated on the Khorat plateau, and the Mekong river borders this part of Thailand with Laos. It is a region unspoiled by mass tourism and is ideal for travellers looking for an authentic travel experience. Check out the amazing prices: Nakorn Phanom has a three star hotel that overlooks the Mekong with a room rate of 850 baht; that's only €21 or $28! If you travel in the northeast, you will discover the warm and friendly Isan people, and their diverse culture and historic heritage. Isan also has breathtaking landscapes, Thai boxing and Isan food, famous all over Thailand for its sticky rice and chillies. And sweet mangoes served with coconut cream! Thank you. Wow, that's hot! Could I try the mango now, please?